R Quick Syntax Reference

T0222585

■ ■ ■

Margot Tollefson

Apress·

R Quick Syntax Reference

Copyright © 2014 by Margot Tollefson

ISBN-13 (pbk): 978-1-4302-6640-2

ISBN-13 (electronic): 978-1-4302-6641-9

President and Publisher: Paul Manning
Acquisitions Editor: Jonathan Hassell
Technical Reviewer: Jessica Orth
Developmental Editor: Robert Hutchinson
Editorial Board: Steve Anglin, Mark Beckner, Ewan Buckingham, Gary Cornell, Louise Corrigan, Jonathan Gennick, Jonathan Hassell, Robert Hutchinson, Michelle Lowman, James Markham, Matthew Moodie, Jeff Olson, Jeffrey Pepper, Douglas Pundick, Ben Renow-Clarke, Dominic Shakeshaft, Gwenan Spearing, Matt Wade
Coordinating Editor: Rita Fernando
Copy Editor: Ann Dickson
Compositor: SPi Global
Indexer: SPi Global
Cover Designer: Anna Ishchenko

Distributed to the book trade worldwide by Springer Science+Business Media New York, 233 Spring Street, 6th Floor, New York, NY 10013. Phone 1-800-SPRINGER, fax (201) 348-4505, e-mail orders-ny@springer-sbm.com, or visit www.springeronline.com. Apress Media, LLC is a California LLC and the sole member (owner) is Springer Science + Business Media Finance Inc (SSBM Finance Inc). SSBM Finance Inc is a **Delaware** corporation.

For information on translations, please e-mail rights@apress.com, or visit www.apress.com.

Apress and friends of ED books may be purchased in bulk for academic, corporate, or promotional use. eBook versions and licenses are also available for most titles. For more information, reference our Special Bulk Sales–eBook Licensing web page at www.apress.com/bulk-sales.

Any source code or other supplementary materials referenced by the author in this text is available to readers at www.apress.com. For detailed information about how to locate your book's source code, go to www.apress.com/source-code/.

To Clay

Contents at a Glance

Contents

About the Author

Margot Tollefson is a self-employed consulting statistician residing in the tiny town of Stratford in the corn and soybean fields of north-central Iowa. She started using the S-Plus language in the early 1990s and happily switched to R about ten years ago. Margot enjoys writing her own functions in R—to do plots and simulations as well as to implement custom modeling and use published statistical methods. She earned her graduate degrees in statistics from Iowa State University in Ames, Iowa.

About the Technical Reviewer

Jessica Orth is a graduate student in the Department of Statistics and Actuarial Science at the University of Iowa. She graduated from the University of Minnesota, Morris, with a degree in statistics in May 2012.

Acknowledgments

I would like to thank the writers of the R Development Core Team at the Comprehensive R Archive Network. Without their help pages, this book could not have been written. I would also like to thank the editors at Apress, Jonathan Hassell, Rita Fernando, and Kevin Shea for guiding my progress; the copy editor, Ann Dickson, for her fine work; Jessica Orth for her helpful comments; and my husband, Clay Conard, for his support and patience over the last few months.

Introduction

R is a programming language that provides the user with powerful data and graphical analysis options. R is both flexible and broad. From tasks as simple as adding two numbers to tasks as complex as fitting an ARIMA model, R is capable of crunching the numbers.

The purpose of *R Quick Syntax Reference* is to provide the reader with the basic syntax of R. Often an R user gets stuck if, for example, a mode is incorrect or a logical test does not work. Because the full spectrum of R packages uses the same fairly simple syntax, *R Quick Syntax Reference* provides the reader with the necessary information to get unstuck and run and create all R functions and code.

The R language is based on the language S, a high-level programming language developed mainly by Richard A. Becker, John M. Chambers, and Allan R. Wilks in the AT&T laboratories in 1975. The R version of the language first became available in 1993 and was developed by Ross Ihaka and Robert Gentleman at the University of Auckland, New Zealand.

R is open source and is a GNU project. As open-source code, the R language is free and constantly being improved. The R Development Core Team currently does the development. Packages for specific analysis techniques are added often. At the present time, there are 4,986 packages available in R. Most users will use only a few packages. Although GUI versions of R are available, we discuss using R at the command prompt in *R Quick Syntax Reference*.

This book is about the S3 version of R—S3 standing for the third version of S, the commercial program on which R is based. The developers of R have a new version, S4—the fourth version of S—running concurrently with S3. Even though version S4 is quite different from S3, it is necessary to know the syntax of S3 in order to use S4. And S3 remains a powerful, flexible language in its own right—hence, this book.

Part I covers the basics of R. Chapter 1 describes how to download and install R for the Windows, Mac, and Linux operating systems and also how to download packages. Because keeping separate folders for different projects is very useful, Chapter 1 gives instructions for running R from different folders. It also gives the methods for updating the R program itself.

Chapter 2 introduces the R prompt, gives a sample calculation, and describes the three parts of R—objects, operators, and assignments. Chapter 3 covers the assignment of names to objects, demonstrates the ls() function that allows you to see the objects in a folder, and discusses the operators in R.

Part II describes R objects. Objects have modes, classes, and types. Chapter 4 lists the modes and describes some of them. It also shows how modes and types differ. Chapter 5 discusses some of the classes.

Part III covers functions. Chapter 6 starts with a list of the 30 default packages in R and follows with instructions on how to use functions. Because packaged functions all have help pages, the chapter provides instructions on how to access and use the help page of a function. Chapter 7 describes how to create a function. Chapter 8 explains how to run a function—with a detailed approach to the argument list.

Part IV focuses on importing and exporting data in R and methods for creating and manipulating some kinds of object. Chapter 9 describes several methods for importing data, gives a number of functions to create data objects, and discusses some random-number generators. Chapter 10 gives several methods for exporting from R. Chapter 11 gives a number of functions that operate on objects—to bind objects together, to find descriptive qualities of an object, to assign qualities to an object, to aggregate an object in some way, or to apply functions to portions of an object.

Part V covers flow conditioning commands and functions. Chapter 12 presents the flow conditioning statements, and Chapter 13 supplies examples of them. Chapter 14 describes the two flow conditioning functions and gives examples.

Part VI discusses functions related to formatting and outputting output, looks at the results from packaged functions and at what some of the default packages contain, and provides some tips for using R. Chapter 15 gives some rounding functions and some functions for outputting from a function. It also gives some functions that vary according to the class of the object on which the function operates and that summarize the results of the function, either textually or visually. Chapter 16 takes a look at the contents of the packages **base**, **stats**, and **graphics** and glances at the **datasets**, **grDevices**, **methods**, and utils packages. Chapter 17 describes how to deal with some common frustrations in R. More information is given on outputting from functions, plus an example of a recursive function and some advice on using R.

PART 1

■ ■ ■

R Basics

Part I introduces you to the basics of the R language.

To use R, you must first download the program from the Internet. Chapter 1 describes how to install R on the Windows, OS X, and Linux operating systems. It also describes how to install and update packages and how to update R and use R within a file system.

Once you've installed and opened R, you are faced with an R prompt and little else. Chapter 2 presents the parts of R (objects, operators, and assignments), the R prompt, and an example of using R as a calculator from the R prompt.

Chapter 3 shows you how to assign names to expressions to create R objects and describes two functions: ls() for listing the objects in the workspace and rm() for removing objects from the workspace. It then discusses the operators that operate on objects and expressions: logical, arithmetic, matrix, relational, and subscripting operators, plus a few other special operators.

CHAPTER 1

■ ■ ■

Downloading R and Setting Up a File System

The first step in using R is to download R from the Internet. R can be downloaded for the modern operating systems Windows, OS X, and Linux. In this chapter, you will learn how to download and install R and the 30 basic packages as well as how to install other packages and update R. You will also learn how to use R in individual folders within the file system of the computer.

Downloading R

You can download R from the web site of the Comprehensive R Archive Network (CRAN). CRAN updates the installation process from time to time; however, the instructions in this book are for the current steps at time of publication. CRAN provides instructions on the web site if the process has changed.

Begin the download process by going to the web site http://cran.r-project.org. At the web site, links to current versions for Windows, OS X, and Linux are listed at the top of the opening window. Select the appropriate link.

Windows

On the page that opens with the Windows link, select the link **base**, which is the top link. In the next window, click on the **download** link for the given Windows version. (Currently, the link is **Download R 3.0.2 for Windows**.) If R has not already been installed on the computer, the downloader will create a default folder in the **Documents** folder to hold R files. Unless there is a reason to change the folder name or location, accept the default. R will begin to download.

When the program finishes downloading, find the downloaded file in your file system. Downloads are put in C://Users/User_folder/Downloads, where **User_folder** is the folder of the user, unless another folder was specified earlier in the installation. Click on the downloaded file, which is an .exe installation file (currently R-3.0.2-win.exe.) A question about the safety of the program may pop up. The installation program is safe, so run the program.

The installation wizard will open. The installation process steps through several pages. On the first page, read the GNU GENERAL PUBLIC LICENSE; then click on **Next**. For the rest of the pages, accepting the defaults on each page is fine, so click on **Next** on each page.

At the page of additional choices, click on **Next**, and the program will begin to install. When the installation is finished, click on **Finish** to complete the installation. The program and the 30 base packages are now installed. An icon for R will be on the computer desktop and, for Windows 8, in the charms. To run R, click on the icon or charm.

OS X

On the page that opens from the OS X link, first read the section under **R for Mac OS X**. The R project gives the advice to check the files for viruses and other problems.

Under **Files:** there are two package choices: the current version and latest version. Selecting the current version (the .pkg link, currently R-3.0.2.pkg) will download both packages. When the packages have finished downloading, open the download box on the icon bar (the yellow and brown box) or the downloads folder under the username in **Finder**.

Select an R version in the download box. Opening the version will open the installer. With the installer open, click on **Continue** to go to the next page of the installer. Read the message from CRAN; then click **Continue**. Again, read the message from CRAN; then click **Continue**.

On the next page, you will find the license. After reading the license, click **Agree** to download R. On the next page, select either of the choices; then click on **Continue**. (The **Continue** button will not light up until a choice is made.)

On the next page, select **Install**. The installation program will ask for a password. After you have entered a password, the installation will begin. When the installation is finished, click on **Close**. R will now be in the applications folder and on the dock and the 30 base packages will be loaded. Select **R** on the dock or in the applications folder to start R.

Linux

At the CRAN site, CRAN provides source code for R for the Linux distributions Debian, Red Hat, Suse, and Ubuntu. The developers state that R is available through the package management system for most distributions of Linux.

If the command line version of R is not available using the package management system, installing R directly from the terminal is an option. At http://cran.r-project.org/bin/linux/distribution, where *distribution* is Debian, Suse, or Ubuntu, you can find instructions for installing R from the terminal command prompt under the ReadMe files.

For Red Hat, http://cran.r-project.org/bin/linux/redhat, there is no ReadMe file. Follow instructions on the CRAN site to install R for Red Hat. Once you have installed R, command line R will be available by typing **R** in the terminal window.

Installing and Updating Packages

When initially installed, R comes with 30 packages. Often the user will want to use the power of the many other packages available in R. Installing and updating a package is straightforward.

For any of the operating systems, if the name of a package is known, typing

```
install.packages("package name")
```

at the R command prompt, where *package name* is the name of the package, will install the package. To update packages, typing

```
update.packages()
```

at the R command prompt will find those packages with updates and update the packages. To see which packages are already installed on the computer, enter

```
installed.packages()
```

at the R prompt.

If the name of the package is not known (also for known names), using the installer for the operating systems Windows and OS X is easy. For Linux, instructions can be found at the CRAN web site, http://cran.r-project.org. Here you can find instructions for Windows and OS X.

Windows

To install a package in Windows not using the command line, start by opening R. On the menu bar at the top of the screen, select **Packages**. A menu will drop down. Select **Install package (s)...**. Either the CRAN mirror window or the Packages window will come up. If the CRAN mirror window comes up, select a close mirror and click **OK**, which will bring up the Packages window.

The Packages window consists of a list of all of the available packages. Scroll down the list to find the package(s) you wish to install and select the package(s). Click on **OK** to begin the installation. As the installation proceeds, the steps of the installation will scroll on the R console. When the R prompt returns to the screen, the installation is complete.

To update packages not using the command line, select **Packages** on the menu bar and then select **Update packages...**. The Packages window to be updated will open, and it will have a list of all of the installed packages with updates. If there are none, the window will be empty. Choose the packages for updating and click on the **OK** button. If a question about using a personal library pops up, choose **Yes**. The packages will update. When the R prompt returns to the screen, the updates are complete.

OS X

To install packages in OS X, start by opening R. On the menu bar at the top of the screen, select **Packages & Data**. From the drop-down menu, select **Package Installer**, which brings up the R Package Installer. Click on **Get List** for a full list of packages or use the **Package Search** option to search for a package. Under either option, select the package(s) to be installed from the list.

Below the list of packages are choices for the location to put the packages. Hover over the list of location options for more information. Usually, one of the first two options will be correct. To the right of the location options are the **Install Selected** and **Update All** buttons. Before clicking on **Install Selected**, check the **Install Dependencies** box to make sure that any necessary packages are installed. Click on **Install Selected** to start the installation process. The selected packages will install.

To update packages, select **Packages & Data** from the menu bar at the top of the screen. From the drop-down menu, select **Package Installer**, which opens up the R Package Installer. At the bottom right of the Installer, select **Update All** and follow instructions.

Updating R

Since CRAN does not provide automatic updates for R, you must update it manually. The processes for Windows and OS X are easy. For the Linux distributions Debian, Suse, and Ubuntu, instructions can be found in the ReadMe files at http://cran.r-project/bin/linux/distribution, where *distribution* is either Debian, Suse, or Ubuntu. For Red Hat Linux, look elsewhere on the CRAN web site.

Windows

The first step in updating R in Windows is to open R and install the package **installr** if the package has not already been installed. Next, use the function **library** to provide access to **installr**. Type

```
library(installr)
```

at the command prompt and press **enter**. Then, to update R, type

```
updateR()
```

at the command prompt and press **enter**. R will either do an update or give a message that the program is up-to-date and return **False**.

Once **installr** has been installed, **installr** does not need to be installed again. The library must be accessed every time R is run.

OS X

The first step in updating R in OS X is to open R and select **R** from the menu bar at the top of the page. To run the updater, select **Check for R Updates** in the drop-down menu under **R** and follow instructions.

Using R in Separate Folders

Separate workspace images for R can be maintained in separate folders for Windows, OS X, and Linux. This property of R is very handy for using R on separate projects. While the process of opening R in a given folder varies by the operating system, once in a folder, saving the workspace image is straightforward. When closing an R session, the program asks if the user would like to save the workspace image. If **Yes** is selected, then .RData and .Rhistory (.Rapp.history for OS X) files are saved in the current directory. (For OS X, the files are hidden, but the files are there.)

The .RData file contains the objects that were in R at the beginning of the session plus any objects that were added during the session minus any objects that were erased during the session. The .Rhistory (.Rapp.history for OS X) file contains the history of the lines input at the R console. By default, all lines up to the last 512 lines are saved in Windows. For OS X and Linux, the default is 250 lines. Access to the lines carries over from session to session if the history is saved.

Windows

To initially set up R in a folder, open R at the desktop. (Click on the **R** icon on the desktop or click on **R** in the list of programs or, in Windows 8, the list of charms.) Select **File** on the menu bar at the top of the screen. From the drop-down menu, select **Change dir...**. The **Browse to folder** window will open. Navigate to the folder of choice.

When exiting R, save the workspace image and R will create .RData and .Rhistory files in the folder. The .RData file will have a blue **R** icon associated with the file. In the future, going to the folder and clicking on the **R** icon will open R and the history and objects saved within the folder will be present.

As a note for the initial setup, any objects in the desktop R will still be in R when the folder is changed. You can easily remove the objects. Type **rm(list=ls())** at the command prompt to remove all objects from the folder.

OS X

Working within different folders in OS X is also easy. There are two ways: dragging and dropping or using the terminal. If R is on the dock and R is not open, dragging the folder from either **Finder** or **Documents** to the **R** icon on the dock will open R in the folder using the .RData and .Rapp.history for that folder.

To open R using the terminal, open the terminal (located under **Applications/ Utilities** in **Finder.**) and type

```
open -a R folder
```

where *folder* is the location of the folder. R will open in the folder using the .RData and .Rapp.history files for that folder.

Linux

To open R in a given folder in Linux, change the directory to the folder and type **R** at the command prompt.

■ ■ ■

CHAPTER 2

The R Prompt

This chapter covers the R prompt. It starts with descriptions of the three parts of R: objects, operators, and assignments. It continues with a discussion of working with the R prompt, followed by an example of doing a calculation at the R prompt.

In Windows and OS X, R runs in GUIs: *RGUI* in Windows and *R.app GUI* in OS X. Both RGUI and R.app GUI open an R Console and run from the R prompt in the R Console. GUIs are available in Linux, but this book covers only running R from the terminal window R prompt.

The Three Parts of R: Objects, Operators, and Assignments

There are basically three parts of R: objects, operators, and assignments.

> *Objects* contain information and can be data, functions, or the results of functions. Objects always have a name. Users create some objects, which are automatically saved on creation. Other objects are functions and datasets contained in the packages of R.

> *Operators* manipulate the objects, numbers, strings, and/or logical variables. For example, entering **a = 2*b** at the R prompt would multiply **b** by two and assign the result to **a**. The objects **a** and **b** are numeric objects and * is the multiplication operator. The equal sign makes an assignment of two times **b** to **a**.

> *Assignments* assign an expression to an object. *Expressions* consist of objects, numbers, logical variables, and/or strings, which are operated on by operators.

Expressions can be evaluated from the R prompt without an assignment. (The other places where assignments and operations occur are within functions and within flow control.)

The R Prompt

All of R flows from the R prompt. R is essentially the running of functions and the doing of calculations. Functions and calculations can be run at the R prompt with or without an assignment to an object. Functions and calculations can also be run as part of a function, but everything starts at the R prompt.

Using R from the R prompt may seem daunting at first. R opens with some script, and then a lonely little greater-than sign (>) is the R prompt. The opening script gives the R version number and some other information about the program, including the fact that the program runs with no warranty.

R remembers every line that is entered into the program, up to a set number of lines. A very handy side of R is that the up and down arrows on the keyboard will step through the lines. You only need to enter an expression once. Corrections to expressions are easy to do without typing the entire expression again.

To close R, enter **q( )** at the R prompt or, for Windows and OS X, close the window. R will close with the option to save the workspace. In Linux, if the terminal window is closed without using **q( )**, the current workspace will be lost.

The workspace consists of any objects present in R at the time the program is closed and the current history. Closing R without saving the workspace will result in reverting to the workspace present at the time the R session started.

An Example of a Calculation

The simplest use of R is as a calculator. The following calculation was done from the R prompt. There is no assignment in the calculation, so the result is returned on the screen.

```
> (1 + 3 + 7)/5
[1] 2.2
>
```

The first line gives the expression to be evaluated and the second line gives the result. The [1] in the second line is a label that tells the user that the result is the first value returned from the expression. Many expressions return more than one value. At the third line, the R prompt comes back and R is ready for another task.

CHAPTER 3

Assignments and Operators

R works with objects. Objects can include vectors, matrices, functions, the results from a function, or a number of other kinds of objects. Objects make working with information easier. This chapter covers assigning names to objects, listing and removing objects, and object operations. Part II (Chapters 4 and 5) covers the possible forms of objects.

Some objects come with the packages in R. Other objects are user-created. User-created objects have names that are assigned by the user. Knowing how to create, list, and remove user-created objects is basic to R.

Types of Assignment

Names in R must begin with a letter or a period, cannot have breaks, and can contain letters, numeric digits, periods, and underscores. The names that begin with a period are hidden and are used by R for startup defaults, the random seed, and other such things. The indexing symbols [],[[]],$, and @ have special meanings with regard to R names, as explained the "Subscripting Operators" section of this chapter.

R originally used five types of assignment, four of which are still current. The four types are

a <- b,

which assigns **b** to **a**,

a -> b,

which assigns **a** to **b**,

a <<- b,

which assigns **b** to **a** and can be used inside a function to bring the assignment up to the workspace level, and

a ->> b,

which assigns **a** to **b** and brings an assignment in a function up to the workspace level.

Recently, the developers at R have included the more standard

```
a = b,
```

which assigns **b** to **a**. While any of the types of assignment can be used, the use of the equal sign is easiest to type.

When R makes an assignment, the name is automatically saved in the workspace. Note that no warning is given if the assigned name already exists. The assignment will overwrite the object in the workspace with the assigned object.

R is interesting in that a function of an object can be assigned to the original object. For example,

```
a = 2*a,
```

where the object **a** is replaced by the original **a** times two.

For more information about assignment operators, enter **?"Assignment Operators"** at the R prompt.

Example of Three Types of Assignment

An example of some of the types of assignment follows. Three objects are created: **abc**, **bcd**, and **cde**. You create the objects by assigning sequences to the objects. The sequences are generated when you put a colon between two integers, which creates a sequence of integers starting with the first integer and ending with the second integer.

To show that the objects actually contain the assigned sequence, the contents of the three objects are displayed below. Note that entering the name of an object at the R prompt will always display the contents of the object. The **[1]** refers to the first element of the objects.

```
> abc = 1:10

> abc
 [1]  1  2  3  4  5  6  7  8  9 10

> bcd <- 11:20

> bcd
 [1] 11 12 13 14 15 16 17 18 19 20

> 21:30 -> cde

> cde
 [1] 21 22 23 24 25 26 27 28 29 30
```

As you can see, the assignment operators <- and = give the same result. The assignment operator -> works in the opposite direction.

The ls() and rm() Functions

To see the objects present in the workspace, use the function ls(). Entering **ls()** at the R prompt for the above example gives

```
> ls()
[1] "abc" "bcd" "cde"
>,
```

which are the three objects created above.

Although functions are covered in detail in Part III, one interesting property of functions to note here is they can have arguments that the user enters. Two of the possible arguments for ls() are **pattern** and **all.names**.

The first argument is entered as **pattern = "a string"**, where *"a string"* is any part of an object name. For example, in the above workspace, searching for those objects containing **bc** in the name gives **abc** and **bcd**, that is

```
> ls(pattern="bc")
[1] "abc" "bcd"
```

The argument **pattern** can be reduced to **pat**, as in **ls(pat="bc")**. The shortening of arguments of functions is a property of R. All arguments in R can be reduced to the shortest unique form, but they are usually given in the full form in manuals.

The second argument is **all.names=**, which can equal **TRUE** or **FALSE**. If set to **TRUE**, the **all.names** argument instructs R to list all of the files in the workspace, including those that begin with a period. **FALSE** is the default value and does not need to be entered. For the example workspace above, setting **all.names** equal to **TRUE** gives

```
> ls(all.n=T)
[1] ".commander.done" ".First"        ".Random.seed"   ".Traceback"
[5] "abc"             "bcd"           "cde"
.
```

The **[1]** refers to ".commander.done" since "commander.done" is the first element of the vector, and the **[5]** refers to "abc" since "abc" is the fifth element of the vector. In R, if the elements of a vector have not been given a name, the convention for listing the elements is to show the index of the first element in each line of the lines of listed elements.

The function rm() can be used to remove objects from the workspace. For rm(), the names of the objects to be deleted are put within the parentheses and separated by commas. For example,

```
rm(a,b,c)
```

will remove objects **a**, **b**, and **c**. To remove all objects,

```
rm(list=ls())
```

works.

For more information about ls() or rm(), enter **?ls** or **?rm** at the R prompt.

Operators

Operators operate on objects. Operators can be logical, arithmetic, matrix, relational, or subscripting, or they may have a special meaning. Each of the types of operators is described here.

For operators, *elementwise* refers to performing the operation on each element of an object or paired elements for two objects. If two objects do not have the same dimensions, the operator will cycle the smaller object against the larger object. The cycling proceeds through each dimension. For example, for matrices the first dimension is the rows and the second dimension is the columns, so the cycling is down rows starting with the first column.

The letters **NA** are used to indicate that an element is missing data. Most operators have rules for dealing with missing data and may return an **NA** if data is missing.

CRAN gives a help page of information about operation precedence. Enter **??"Operator Syntax and Precedence"** at the R prompt to see the page.

Logical Operators and Functions

Logical operators return the values **TRUE**, **FALSE**, or **NA**, where **NA** refers to a missing value. The logical operators are the **not** operator, two **or** operators, two **and** operators, the **exclusive or** function (which is a function that acts as an operator), and the **any** function (which is a function that operates on a logical object). For logical operators, if the two objects do not have the same dimensions, the number of elements in the larger object must be a multiple of the number of elements in the smaller object for cycling to occur. The logical operators and two logical functions are listed in Table 3-1.

Table 3-1. *The Logical Operators and Functions*

Operator	Operation	Description
!	not	negation operator—e.g., !a
|	or	elementwise **or** operator—e.g., a|b
||	or	**or** operator, just evaluates the first elements in the objects—e.g., a||b
&	and	elementwise **and** operator—e.g., a&b
&&	and	**and** operator, just evaluates the first elements in the objects—e.g., a&&b
xor()	exclusive or	**exclusive or** function—e.g., xor(a,b)
any()	logical test	tests if **TRUE** is present in a logical object—e.g., any(a)

The logical operators operate on objects that are logical, numeric, or raw. When a numeric object is coerced to logical, all of the nonzero values are set to **TRUE** and the zero values are set to **FALSE**. For raw vectors, the operators are applied bitwise.

The negation operator changes **TRUE** to **FALSE** and **FALSE** to **TRUE** in a logical object. The operator | compares the two objects elementwise and, for each pair of elements, returns **TRUE** if **TRUE** is present, and **FALSE** otherwise. The operator || compares the first element of the first object to the first element of the second object and returns **TRUE** if **TRUE** is present, or **FALSE** otherwise.

The operator & compares two objects elementwise and, for each pair of elements, returns **TRUE** if both elements are **TRUE**, and **FALSE** otherwise. The operator **&&** compares the first element of the first object to the first element of the second object and returns **TRUE** if the first elements are both **TRUE**, otherwise **FALSE**.

The xor() function compares objects elementwise and returns **TRUE** if the paired elements are different and **FALSE** if the paired elements are the same.

For a logical vector or a vector that can be coerced to logical, the function any() will return **TRUE** if any of the elements are **TRUE**, and **FALSE** otherwise.

For more information about the logical operators, the CRAN help pages for logical operators can be found by entering **??"logical operators"** at the R prompt. The help page for any() can be accessed by entering **?any** at the R prompt.

Arithmetic Operators

Arithmetic operators can have numeric operands or operands that can be coerced to numeric. For example, for logical objects **TRUE** coerces to **1** and **FALSE** coerces to **0**. For some types of objects, specific operators have a different meaning, but those types of objects will not be covered in this chapter.

Arithmetic expressions are evaluated elementwise. If the number of elements is not the same between the objects in an expression, the smaller object cycles through the larger one until the end of the larger one. The numbers of elements in the larger object do not have to be a multiple of the smaller object for cycling. Expressions are evaluated from left to right, under the rules of precedence.

The arithmetic operators are the standard * for multiplication, / for division, + for addition, and - for subtraction. The exponentiation symbol is ^. The operator %% gives the modulus of the first argument with respect to the second argument. The operator %/% performs integer division. Expressions can be grouped using parentheses, for example **(a+b)/c**. Table 3-2 lists the arithmetic operators.

Table 3-2. *Arithmetic Operators*

Operator	Operation	Example
*	multiplication	a*b
/	division	a/b
+	addition	a+b
-	subtraction	a-b
^	exponentiation	a^b
%%	modulus	a%%b
%/%	integer division	a%/%b

15

For more information, the CRAN help pages for arithmetic operators can be found by entering **??"arithmetic operators"** at the R prompt.

Matrix Operators and Functions

R provides operators and functions to manipulate matrices. A list of some matrix operators and functions can be found in Table 3-3.

Table 3-3. Matrix Operators and Functions

Operator / Function	Operation	Example
%*%	matrix multiplication	a%*%b
%o% or **outer( )**	outer product of two vectors, matrices, or arrays	a%*%b, outer(a,b)
t( )	transpose of a matrix	t(a)
crossprod( ) or **tcrossprod( )**	crossproduct of a matrix or two matrices	crossprod(a) or crossprod(a,b) or tcrossprod(a) or tcrossprod(a,b)
diag( )	diagonal of a matrix or a diagonal matrix	diag(a), **a** is a matrix or diag(a), **a** is a vector
solve()	inverse of a matrix or solution to **Xa=b**	solve(a), solve(X,b)

The matrix multiplication operator is **%*%**. R will return an error if the two matrices do not conform.

For two arrays (arrays include vectors and matrices), **%o%**, or outer(), gives the outer product of the arrays.

To transpose a matrix, use the function t( ), for example, t(a).

To get the cross product of one matrix with another (or the original matrix), use either the function crossprod( ) or the function tcrossprod( ). If **a** and **b** are conforming matrices, then

```
crossprod(a) = t(a)%*%a,

tcrossprod(a) = a%*%t(a),

crossprod(a,b) = t(a)%*%b,

tcrossprod(a,b) = a%*%t(b).
```

To find the inverse of a nonsingular square matrix, use the function solve(), for example, solve(a). The function solve() also can solve the linear equation

Xa=b,

for **a**, where **X** is a nonsingular square matrix and **b** has the same number of rows as **X**. The syntax is solve(X,b).

To create a diagonal matrix or obtain the diagonal of a matrix, use the function diag(). If **a** is a vector, diag(a) will return a diagonal matrix with the diagonal equal to the **a**. For example:

```
> a = 1:2
> a
[1] 1 2

> diag(a)
     [,1] [,2]
[1,]    1    0
[2,]    0    2
```

If **a** is a matrix, diag(a) will return the diagonal elements of the matrix, even if the matrix is not square. For example:

```
> a = matrix(1:6,2,3)

> a
     [,1] [,2] [,3]
[1,]    1    3    5
[2,]    2    4    6

> diag(a)
[1] 1 4
```

For more information, the CRAN help page for matrix multiplication can be found by entering **??"matrix multiplication"** at the R prompt. For the five functions, entering **?name**, where *name* is the name of the function, brings up the help page for the function.

Relational Operators

Relational operators are used in logical tests. The six relational operators are == for equal to, != for not equal to, < for less than, <= for less than or equal to, > for greater than, and >= for greater than or equal to. The list of logical operators can be found in Table 3-4.

Table 3-4. *Logical Operators*

Operator	Operation	Example
==	equals	a==9
!=	not equal	a!=9
>	greater than	a>9
>=	greater than or equal to	a>=9
<	less than	a<9
<=	less than or equal to	a<=9

Note that the **equal to** relational operator is ==, not =. A common mistake is to enter = for == in a logical expression. R will return an error for =.

As with arithmetic operators, logical expressions can be grouped using parentheses. For example,

```
(( a>0 & b>0 ) & ( a<5 & b<5 ))
```

is a logical expression and can be assigned a name.

The CRAN help page for relational operators can be found by entering **??"relational operators"** at the R prompt.

Subscripting Operators

Many objects in R have more than one element. Subscripting is used to access specific elements of an object. Vectors, matrices, arrays, lists, and slots can be subscripted. Single square brackets ([]), double square brackets ([[]]), dollar signs ($) and *at* symbols (@) are used for subscripting. None are used elsewhere.

Vectors

For vectors, using single square brackets is usually appropriate. Double square brackets can also be used, but they can only access a single element of the vector at a time. Within single square brackets, there may be a logical expression or a set of indices. For example:

```
a[ 3:7 ]  or  a[ a>3 ]
```

The first expression results in the third through seventh elements of **a**. The second expression results in those elements of **a** that are greater than three.

If indices are given a negative sign, those indices are not included For example,

```
a[ -2:-6 ]
```

would return the object **a** with elements two through six removed.

An object can be subsetted in one set of square brackets and subsetted again in another set of square brackets. For example:

```
a[1:10][b>3],
```

where the length of **a** is greater than or equal to ten, and **b** is of length ten. The expression would return those elements of the first ten elements of **a** for which the corresponding element of **b** is greater than three. The subsetting can be continued with more sets of square brackets. Each set will operate on the result of all previous subsetting.

Matrices

For matrices, both kinds of square brackets are also used. For single square brackets, the selection instructions for the rows are separated from the selection instructions for the columns by a comma. Like the subsetting for vectors, for single square brackets, indices or a logical expression may be used to subset a matrix. To reference all rows of a matrix, put nothing to the left of the comma inside the brackets. To reference all columns of a matrix, put nothing to the right of the comma inside the brackets.

Double square brackets return just one value. If subsetted with a row and a column index separated by a comma, the value in the cell is returned. If just one index value is entered within double square brackets, R treats the matrix as a vector—going down rows—and returns the indexed element of the vector.

An example of matrix subscripting is

```
a[ a[,1]>3 , 1:4 ],
```

where **a** is a matrix with at least four columns. The expression would return those rows of the first four columns for which the elements of the first column are bigger than three. Notice that the **a[,1]** consists of one column and contains all of the rows.

A matrix can also be subsetted using a matrix with two columns. The two-column matrix would contain row and column indices and would pick out individual cells in the matrix based on the indices in each row. For example, if **b** is a matrix with [1 2] in the first row and [2 3] in the second row, then a[b] would return the two elements a[1,2] and a[2,3].

Arrays

Arrays are like matrices but can have more than two dimensions. Note that a matrix is an array with two dimensions and a vector is an array with one dimension. Subscripting arrays with more than two dimensions is just like subscripting matrices except that, for single square brackets, there are more commas in the brackets. An example is

```
a[ 1:3,,2:7 ],
```

where **a** is a three-dimensional array with at least three levels in the first dimension and at least seven levels in the third dimension. The result of the subsetting would be all of the elements in the second dimension for which the index in the first dimension is one, two, or three and the indices in the third dimension are between two and seven inclusive.

Like matrices, arrays can be subsetted using a matrix that has the same number of columns as the number of dimensions of the array, the rows of which would consist of indices for individual cells of the array.

Lists

Lists are collections of R objects. The objects can be any type of object and do not have to be of the same type within a list. The objects are indexed in the list. To look at objects in a list, single square brackets are used. For example,

```
blist[ 1:5 ]
```

would return the first five objects in **blist** and would also be a list.

To access an object in a list, double square brackets or a dollar sign are required. For example,

```
blist[[2]]
```

would return the second object in the list **blist** and

```
blist$b1
```

would return the object in **blist** with name **b1**. Objects in a list can only be accessed one at a time.

If a list is created from objects that do not have names associated with the objects, names will be given to the objects when the list is created. Names can be changed at any time.

Data frames are a special kind of list. Data frames have the same number of elements for every object in the list and are defined as data.frames. Data frames can be subsetted like a matrix or like a list. If subsetted like a matrix, the resulting object will be a list. If subsetted like a list, the resulting object will be raw, complex, numeric, logical, or character depending on whether the list object is raw, complex, numeric, logical, or character. Individual cells in a data.frame can be accessed using indices in the double square brackets. For example,

```
adframe[[ 1,2 ]]
```

would return the element in the first row and second column of list **adframe**.

Many functions return output in lists. Dollar sign subscripting is usually used to access the output, although square bracket indexing can be used. For example, for the linear model function lm(), entering

```
lm(y~x)$resid
```

or

```
lm(y~x)[[2]]
```

will return the residuals from a simple linear regression of y on x, as will the two sets of statements

```
a=lm(y~x)
a$resid
```

or

```
a=lm(y~x)
a[[2]].
```

Other Types

Two other types of object can be subsetted—factors and slots. Objects that are factors are vectors and can be subsetted like vectors. Slots are a newer type of object and are subsetted using @. More information about subsetting both can be found by entering **??"Extract or Replace"** at the R prompt.

Odds and Ends

Two object systems—S3 and S4—are used in R. Slots are part of S4. S3 and S4 are discussed in Chapter 4 and in the pdf at www.r-project.org/conferences/useR-2004/Keynotes/Leisch.pdf.

Assignments can be done to subsets of an object. For example, let **a** be a matrix and let the user want to change those values in **a** that are greater than 100 to 100. Then the statement

```
a[ a>100 ] = 100
```

will do the replacement and leave the rest of the matrix intact.

The **?** and **??** operators open the help pages. For known function names, **?name** (or **help(name)**) will return the help page for the function, where *name* is the name of the function. To search for functions related to some techniques or methods, the operator, **??** is used. Entering **??"keywords"** (or **help.search("keywords")**), where *keywords* consists of keywords about the technique or method, may give a list of functions in packages related to the topic. Sometimes the search comes up blank. Try again with different keywords.

The colon is used in four ways in R. Of interest here is just the use of a single colon to define a sequence and the double colon to refer to functions by package and name.

If **a** and **b** are two numbers, the expression **a:b** will give the sequence of integers between **a** rounded down to an integer and **b** rounded down to an integer. Note that the number **a** can be larger than the number **b**.

The functions that come with R are all part of some package. If a package is not loaded, a search using just the function name will return nothing. The full name of a function is *package.name::function.name*, where *package.name* is the name of the package and *function name* is the name of the function.

For more information on colons, enter **?":"** at the R prompt.

The operator ~ is used in model formulas to separate the left and right sides of a model. For more information, **type ?"~"** at the R prompt.

The symbol # is used for comments. When writing functions, anything found to the right of a # on a line of the code is ignored.

The CRAN help pages for subsetting are found by entering **??"Extract or Replace"**.

PART 2

■ ■ ■

Kinds of Objects

Part II covers the different kinds of objects that are used in R in terms of their two important qualities: mode and class.

Chapter 4 lists the modes and describes the common ones. In addition to listing all of the modes current in R, the chapter describes the properties of the atomic modes—NULL, raw, logical, numeric, complex, and character—and of the nonatomic modes list, function, call, name, and expression.

Chapter 5 introduces the classes and gives the properties of several of them. The chapter includes a special section on vectors, which are not a class but, a very common kind of object. The classes associated with vectors are raw, logical, integer, double, complex, character, some lists, and expressions. For most atomic objects, the mode and the class are the same. After describing vectors, we give properties of the classes for matrices, arrays, time series, factors, data frames, dates, and times and dates.

Part II concludes with information about assigning names to the dimensions of vectors, matrices, arrays, and lists.

Kinds of Objects

■ ■ ■

Modes of Objects

R objects exist within an object system. R has two object systems: S3 and S4. S4 is the newest version of R and contains a new way to approach R programming. S3 is the preceding version. Both versions run concurrently. S4 offers powerful new methods, but to use those methods a solid knowledge of S3 is necessary. This book focuses mainly on S3 methods, including S4 syntax where appropriate.

Overview of the Modes

Modes describe the type of information an object contains and are an S3-level classification. The mode of an object can be found by using the function mode(). The S4 level classification is by type and can be found using the function typeof(). Currently, R objects fall into one of the following modes: NULL, logical, numeric, complex, raw, character, list, expression, name, function, pairlist, language, char, ..., environment, externalptr, weakref, closure, bytecode, promise, and S4. Since R is constantly changing, the list of modes may change. With a few exceptions, the types and the modes are the same and most of the modes can be found under the list of types. The list of types can be found at the help page for typeof() and at http://svn.r-project.org/R/trunk/src/main/util.c, under the TypeTable. The instances for which mode() and typeof() give different results include the following: the function typeof() returns either integer or double where mode() returns numeric, typeof() returns either special or built-in where mode() returns function, and typeof() returns symbol where mode() returns name. The help page for mode() gives the cross reference between modes and types.

Commonly Used Modes

Most users will never use half of the modes. The commonly used modes are NULL, logical, numeric, complex, raw, character, list, function, call, name, expression, and S4. The mode NULL is the mode of an otherwise modeless empty object. Objects of mode logical contain elements that can take on the values **TRUE, FALSE,** or **NA,** where **NA** represents a missing value. Objects of mode numeric can take on integer or real numeric values or **NA**s. Objects of mode complex can take on complex numeric values or **NA**s. Objects of mode raw are made up of bytes. **NA**s are set to **00** for raw data.

Objects of mode character are made up of character strings or **NA**s. The elements of character objects are quoted, except for **NA**s. Objects of mode list are lists of other objects, which can be of any mode. Objects of mode function are functions. Objects of mode name are a simplified name of an object based on the first element of the object, assuming the first element is not missing. Objects of mode call are functions and arguments. Objects of mode expression are collections of objects such as calls and names. Objects of mode S4 are those S4 objects that are complex (referring to the structure of the object, not to complex numbers).

The sources for the preceding information are the help pages for mode() and typeof().

Atomic, Recursive, and Language Modes

Modes come in three kinds: atomic, recursive, and language. The atomic modes are NULL, logical, numeric, complex, raw, and character. *Atomic* refers to the elements of the objects being atomlike. For the atomic modes, all of the elements within the object are of the same atomic mode. Recursive modes are collections of objects and can contain objects of different modes. Two types of recursive modes are list and function. Most objects that are not atomic are recursive. The language modes are name, call, and expression. More information about the kinds of modes can be found under the help pages for the functions that test for the kind of mode of an object: is.atomic(), is.recursive(), and is.language().

Some Functions for Atomic Modes

Each of the atomic modes, except NULL, has three functions associated with the mode: the function named for the mode, name(); an as.name() function; and an is.name() function, where *name* is the name of the mode. The name() function creates a vector of the length given by the argument or arguments, if the argument(s) are of the correct mode and permissible value(s).

The as.name() function attempts to coerce the argument of the function to the named mode. If the coercion is not possible, the as.name() function returns a vector of **NA**s or gives an error. Note that if the argument is a matrix or array, a vector of the elements of the matrix or array will be returned, where the conversion to a vector proceeds down each dimension of the matrix or array in turn (in the case of a matrix, going down the rows of the first column, then the second column, and so on).

The is.name() function tests whether the argument of the function is of the named mode and returns **TRUE** or **FALSE**, depending on whether the argument is or is not.

The NULL Mode

NULL is a reserved object in R and is also a mode. While there is no function NULL() in R, as.null() and is.null() are functions. With any object used as an argument or with no argument, as.null() returns just one NULL. The function is.null() returns **TRUE** if the argument is equal to **NULL**; **FALSE** otherwise.

The Logical Mode

The function logical() with no argument or with zero for an argument returns logical(0), which is the logical empty set and has length zero. The function logical() with an integer greater than zero as an argument returns a vector of **FALSE**s of length equal to the integer. If the argument is a single double precision element, the element is rounded down and a vector of **FALSE**s of the length equal to the resulting integer is created. If the argument is a numeric object other than a single number or if the argument is a logical object, the function returns **FALSE**. If the argument is of mode NULL, character, complex, raw, or a nonatomic mode, then logical() gives an error.

The function as.logical() coerces the argument of the function to logical, if possible, and returns a vector containing **TRUE**s, **FALSE**s, and/or **NA**s. If there is no argument or the argument is zero or **NULL**, as.logical() returns logical(0), a logical empty set of length zero. If the argument is of mode numeric, zeroes will be returned as **FALSE**s and all other numbers will be returned as **TRUE**s.

If the argument is a complex object, the function returns **FALSE** for 0+0i and **TRUE** for any other complex number. If the mode is raw, 00s will return **FALSE** and any other value will return **TRUE**. If the argument is of mode character, the function returns a vector of **NA**s of length equal to the length of the argument. If the argument contains **NA**s, for any of the modes except raw, **NA**s will be returned for the elements containing **NA**s. For the raw mode, there are no **NA**s since **NA**s are interpreted as 00s in the raw mode. For any other mode, as.logical() gives an error.

The function is.logical() returns **TRUE** if the argument is a logical object and **FALSE** otherwise. The result of is.logical(logical(0)) is **TRUE**.

For more information about the logical mode, enter ?logical at the R prompt.

The Numeric Mode

For the mode numeric, things get a bit complicated. Originally in S, numeric objects could be integer, real, or double (for double precision). The real option is deprecated and should not be used. In S3, the integer and double options are both under mode numeric. In S4, each has a separate type. The functions numeric(), is.numeric(), and as.numeric() ae covered here. The functions integer(), as.integer(), is.integer(), double(), as.double(), and is.double() behave similarly but are not covered here because they are at the S4 level.

The function numeric() takes a numeric object or NULL as an argument. If the argument equals zero or NULL or there is no argument, numeric() returns numeric(0), an empty object of mode numeric and length zero. If a numeric object of length greater than one or a logical object is the argument, only the first element is evaluated. For a logical argument, **TRUE** is coerced to one and **FALSE** is coerced to zero, while for a numeric argument, the first element is rounded down to an integer. The function then returns a vector on zeroes of length equal to the value of the first element. For arguments of modes other than numeric or logical, R returns an error.

The function as.numeric() attempts to coerce an object to double precision. The argument can be any atomic mode object. If the argument is NULL or no argument is given, numeric(0) is returned, where numeric(0) is an empty object of type numeric and length zero. If the object is logical, **TRUE**s are set to one and **FALSE**s are set to zero in

27

the object. If the object is numeric, the values of the elements are returned as double precision numbers. If the object is complex, only the real parts are returned—as double precision numbers. If the object is of mode raw, as.numeric() converts the hexadecimal values to double precision. If the object is of mode character, the function returns **NA**s for the elements of the object. If the argument is not atomic, R gives an error. Elements with a value of **NA** are returned as **NA**.

The function is.numeric() tests an object to see if the object is a numeric object and works with objects of any mode. The value **TRUE** is returned if the object is numeric and **FALSE** otherwise.

More information about mode numeric objects can be found by entering **?numeric** at the R prompt.

The Complex Mode

The complex mode is the mode of complex numbers. Complex numbers can be created using complex() or by simply typing in the numbers at the R prompt. For example:

```
> a = complex(real=1:5, imaginary=6:10)
> a
[1] 1+ 6i 2+ 7i 3+ 8i 4+ 9i 5+10i

> a = 1:5 + 1i*6:10
> a
[1] 1+ 6i 2+ 7i 3+ 8i 4+ 9i 5+10i
```

Note that for complex numbers there is always a number with no operator in front of the **i**, which lets R know that the **i** is the imaginary root of minus one.

For the function complex(), an argument of zero or no argument returns complex(0), an empty set of mode complex and length zero. If the argument is a single positive number, complex() returns a vector of complex zeroes of the length of the number rounded down to an integer. If the argument consists of a numeric object with more than one element or if the argument is logical either with one element or more than one element, only the first element of the argument is used, where for logical objects **FALSE** is coerced to zero and **TRUE** to one.

The function complex() also take the arguments **real** and **imaginary** or **modulus** and **argument**. The arguments **real** and **imaginary** or **modulus** and **argument** can be set equal to any numeric or logical objects. The objects do not have to be the same length and will cycle. The arguments **real** and **imaginary** are the real and imaginary parts of the numbers while the arguments **modulus** and **argument** are the polar coordinates of the numbers, with **modulus** equal to the lengths of the numbers and **argument** equal to the angles above the x axis of the numbers in radians.

Numbers of mode raw can be used for the **real** and **imaginary** arguments and will be changed to double precision, but they cannot be used for the **modulus** and **argument** arguments. For the **real** and **imaginary** pair, either one can be omitted, and the omitted argument will be set to zero. For the **modulus** and **argument** pair, if **modulus** is omitted, the value for **modulus** will be set to one, and if **argument** is omitted, the value for **argument** will be set to zero. Some examples of complex() include the following:

```
> complex(real=c(T,F), imaginary=1:5+0.5)
[1] 1+1.5i 0+2.5i 1+3.5i 0+4.5i 1+5.5i

> complex(modulus=c(1,2), argument=pi/4)
[1] 0.7071068+0.7071068i 1.4142136+1.4142136i

> as.raw(27:30)
[1] 1b 1c 1d 1e

> complex(real=as.raw(27:30))
[1] 27+0i 28+0i 29+0i 30+0i

> complex(ima=as.raw(27:30))
[1] 0+27i 0+28i 0+29i 0+30i

> complex(mod=as.raw(27:30))
Error in rep_len(modulus, n) * exp((0+1i) * rep_len(argument, n)) :
  non-numeric argument to binary operator

> complex(mod=3:5)
[1] 3+0i 4+0i 5+0i

> complex(arg=3:5*pi/180)
[1] 0.9986295+0.0523360i 0.9975641+0.0697565i 0.9961947+0.0871557i
```

The function as.complex( ) will try to coerce an object to mode complex. If the object can be coerced to numeric (the atomic modes) but is not complex, then the result is a complex object with the coerced argument as the real part and with zeros for the imaginary part, except for **NAs**, which are returned simply as **NAs**. For nonatomic modes, as.complex() returns an error.

The function is.complex() tests whether the argument to the function is of mode complex. The function returns **TRUE** if the argument is of the complex mode and **FALSE** otherwise.

More information about the complex mode can be found by entering **?complex** at the R prompt.

The Raw Mode

The raw mode is for bytewise analysis. The numbers in a raw object are in hexadecimal format, with each element consisting of two digits, either of which can take on any of the values zero through nine or **a** through **f**. Raw elements cannot have a decimal equivalent of greater than 255 (that is, be a hexadecimal number with more than two digits) or be negative.

The function raw() returns a vector of **00**s of length specified by the argument. If no argument or an argument of zero is given, raw() returns raw(0), an raw empty set with length zero. If a single number is entered as the argument, raw() returns a vector of length equal to the number rounded down to an integer. If any other kind of object is entered as the argument, raw() gives an error.

The function as.raw() attempts to coerce the argument of the function to raw. If no argument is given, as.raw() returns an error. If the argument is **NULL**, as.raw() returns raw(0), the raw empty set. If the argument is zero, the function returns **00**, the hexadecimal zero.

Objects of any of the atomic modes can be used as arguments for as.raw(). For logical mode objects, **FALSE**s are set to **00** and **TRUE**s are set to **01**. For numeric mode objects, for values greater than or equal to zero and less than 256, the numbers are rounded down to an integer and converted to hexadecimal. Numbers outside the legal range are converted to **00**. For objects of mode complex, the real portion is treated in the same way as numeric objects and the imaginary portion is discarded. For objects of mode character, all of the elements are converted to **00**. Any element equal to **NA** will also be set to **00**. Using objects of modes other than atomic modes for the argument gives an error.

The function is.raw() tests if an object is of mode raw. The function returns **TRUE** if the object is of mode raw and **FALSE** otherwise. Any object can be used as an argument to is.raw().

More information about the mode raw can be found by entering **?raw** at the R prompt.

The Character Mode

Character mode objects are made up of quoted strings. If an object is text, the text will be broken at each 500 characters to form a vector of strings. The three usual functions also apply to the character mode.

The function character() creates a vector of empty strings and only takes mode numeric, one-element arguments. If the argument is greater than or equal to one, the argument is rounded down to an integer and the function returns a vector of ""s of length equal to the integer. If the argument is less than one and greater than or equal to zero, the character empty set of length zero, character(0), is returned. Other arguments return an error.

The function as.character() tries to convert the argument to strings. For the atomic modes, the conversion is literal, but the elements are returned within quotes. For double precision numbers up to 15 significant digits are used. Unlike the other atomic modes—except NULL—the function as.character() also returns results for some of the recursive modes.

Objects of mode list are described under the next section. In this section, lists are collections of objects that can be of any mode. The function lm() used in the example below fits a linear regression model, with the value to the left of the tilde being the dependent variable and the value to the right the independent variable. The output from lm() is a list.

With an object of mode list as an argument, as.character() may return some strange things depending on the list. The function may return something different from what is returned if the argument is entered at the R prompt. Examples follow:

```
> a.list
[[1]]
     a1 a2 a3 a4
[1,]  1  6 11 16
[2,]  2  7 12 17
[3,]  3  8 13 18
[4,]  4  9 14 19
[5,]  5 10 15 20

[[2]]
 [1]  1  2  3  4  5  6  7  8  9 10

[[3]]
[1] "glh" "abc"


> as.character(a.list)
[1] "1:20"              "1:10"              "c(\"glh\", \"abc\")"

> a.lm

Call:
lm(formula = y ~ x)

Coefficients:
(Intercept)            x
          1            1

> as.character(a.lm)
 [1] "c(0.999999999999999, 1)"
 [2] "c(0, 0, 0)"
 [3] "c(-5.19615242270663, -1.41421356237309, 0)"
 [4] "2"
 [5] "c(2, 3, 4)"
 [6] "0:1"
 [7] "list(qr = c(-1.73205080756888, 0.577350269189626, 0.577350269189626,
-3.46410161513776, -1.41421356237309, 0.965925826289068), qraux =
c(1.57735026918963, 1.25881904510252), pivot = 1:2, tol = 1e-07, rank = 2)"
 [8] "1"
 [9] "list()"
[10] "lm(formula = y ~ x)"
[11] "y ~ x"
[12] "list(y = 2:4, x = 1:3)"
```

Play around with different kinds of lists to see how as.character() performs. Objects of modes name, call, and expression can also be coerced to character. Objects of modes function and S4 cannot.

The function is.character() tests to see if the argument to the function is of mode character and returns **TRUE** if so and **FALSE** otherwise. Any object can be used as an argument.

For more information about the character mode, enter **?character** at the R prompt.

The Common Recursive and Language Modes

The recursive and language modes covered in this book are list, function, call, expression, and name. The modes list, function, call, and expression are all recursive modes. The modes call and expression are also language modes. The mode name is a language mode but not a recursive mode.

The List Mode

Lists are collections of objects, which may be of any mode and which do not have to be of the same mode within the list. The list mode has the same three functions as the atomic modes; however, there are a few more. Creating an empty list differs from the atomic modes. To create a list of a given number of objects where the objects are **NULL**s, use

```
vector("list", n),
```

where **n** is the number of objects to be in the list. The variable, **n**, must be numeric, is rounded down to an integer, and can only contain one element.

The function unlist() removes the list property for some lists and, for those lists, returns a vector of the elements of the objects in the list.

The function alist() creates a list where the values of variables in the list do not have to be specified. The function alist() is most often used in evaluating functions, where some variables can be prespecified and others are assigned at each running of the function.

The function list() creates a list out of the arguments to the function. Within the parentheses, the arguments are separated by commas. The arguments can be any kind of object.

The function as.list() attempts to coerce the argument to mode list. If more than one argument is supplied, only the first argument is coerced. The other arguments are ignored.

The function is.list() tests if the argument is a list (or a pairwise list, which is not covered here). If the object is of mode list, **TRUE** is returned. Otherwise, **FALSE** is returned.

More information can be found by entering **?list** at the R prompt, which brings up the help page for list().

The Function Mode

Functions in R are of mode function. Of the functions listed for atomic modes, only is.function() and function() exist for the mode function. The function is.function() returns **TRUE** if the argument is a function and **FALSE** otherwise. The function function() creates functions, but the structure of functions is different from the atomic modes and the list mode, and the help page for function() is different from the help page for is.function(). We will cover the creation of functions in Chapter 7.

Another mode for functions is closure. The mode closure is for functions that are not primitive—that is, are written in R code. Note that functions of mode closure are also of mode function. The function is.primitive() exists to test if a function is primitive, but a function is.closure() does not exist.

More information about the function mode can be found by entering **?is.function** at the R prompt, which will bring up the help page for is.function().

The Call Mode

Objects of the call mode are unevaluated functions with arguments, if the function takes arguments. The same three functions that exist for the atomic modes exist for the call mode: call(), as.call(), and is.call().

The function call() creates an object of mode call. The first argument of call() is the name of the function in quotes. The rest of the arguments to call are the arguments to the function. Some examples include the following:

```
> a.call = call("lm", y~x)
> a.call
lm(y ~ x)

> b.call = call("ls")
> b.call
ls()

> c.call = call("ls", pattern="abc")
> c.call
ls(pattern = "abc")
```

Note that an object of mode call can be evaluated using the function eval(). If all of the variables in the call exist in the workspace, eval() will evaluate the function; otherwise eval() will give an error. For example:

```
> x
[1] 1 2 3
> y
[1] 2 3 4
> eval(a.call)
```

```
Call:
lm(formula = y ~ x)

Coefficients:
(Intercept)            x
          1            1

> a.call = call("lm", z~x)
>
> z
Error: object 'z' not found
>
> eval(a.call)
Error in eval(expr, envir, enclos) : object 'z' not found
```

The function as.call() tries to coerce the argument to an object of mode call. If the argument is a list, then the conversion takes place; otherwise an error is returned. However, if the list does not consist of the name of a function followed by the arguments of that function, the object cannot be evaluated.

The function is.call() tests the argument and returns **TRUE** if the argument is of mode call and **FALSE** otherwise.

Further information about the mode call can be found by **entering ?call** at the R prompt.

The Name Mode

The mode name refers to objects that are names created for and from other objects. Only the functions as.name() and is.name() exist for the name mode. Names can be up to 10,000 bytes long.

The function as.name() takes arguments that can be logical, numeric, complex, raw, character, or name. Arguments of other modes give an error. The function uses the first element of the object to assign the name. For example:

```
> mat
      one two
row1    1   6
row2    2   7

> as.name(mat)
`1`.
```

The function is.name() tests if the argument is of mode name and returns **TRUE** if so and **FALSE** otherwise.

Note that the mode name and the type symbol are the same so as.name() is the same as as.symbol() and is.name() is the same as is.symbol(). The mode name is the S3 convention and the type symbol is the S4 convention. More information can be found by entering **?name** at the R prompt.

The Expression Mode

The expression mode is like the list mode, but mainly for objects of modes like class or name. Objects of mode expression can be subsetted like lists and are not evaluated when created. The expression mode uses the three functions that the atomic modes use: expression(), as.expression(), and is.expression().

The function expression() creates a listing of the objects entered into the function. The objects are separated by commas and can be of any mode. The function eval() can be used to evaluate the expression. Only the last object in an expression is evaluated under eval(). If the last argument is made up of primitive functions, eval() will return the result, while if the function or expression is not primitive, eval() will return the expression. A second eval() is then necessary to evaluate the function or expression. Examples follow:

```
> a.exp = expression(sin(1:5/180*pi))
> a.exp
expression(sin(1:5/180 * pi))
> eval(a.exp)
[1] 0.01745241 0.03489950 0.05233596 0.06975647 0.08715574

> a.exp = expression(sin(1:5/180*pi),a.call)
> a.exp
expression(sin(1:5/180 * pi), a.call)
> eval(a.exp)
lm(y ~ x)
> eval(eval(a.exp))

Call:
lm(formula = y ~ x)

Coefficients:
(Intercept)              x
          1              1

> a.exp = expression(a.call,sin(1:5/180*pi))
> eval(a.exp)
[1] 0.01745241 0.03489950 0.05233596 0.06975647 0.08715574
```

An object of name mode will give an error if placed as the last argument in an expression that is being evaluated.

The function as.expression() attempts to coerce the argument to mode expression. The modes NULL, call, name, and pairlist are coerced to a single element expression. Atomic modes other than NULL are coerced elementwise. Lists are coerced with no changes except the mode. Other modes of objects will give an error if coercion is attempted.

The function is.expression() tests the argument and will return **TRUE** if the argument is of mode expression and **FALSE** otherwise.

More information about the expression mode can be found by entering
?expression at the R prompt.

The S4 Mode

The mode S4 identifies objects that are used in the new S4 version of R, which uses a
quite different syntax and is not covered in this book. The isS4() function returns **TRUE**
if an object is of mode S4 and **FALSE** otherwise. The function mode() returns **S4** if the
argument is of mode *S4*.

You can find more information by entering **?S4** at the R prompt.

CHAPTER 5

■ ■ ■

Classes of Objects

In R, objects belong to classes as well as modes and types. Classes tell something about how an object is structured. S3 and S4 differ with regard to classes. In S3, there are specific classes into which an R objects falls. In S4, the user defines a class for an S4 object. Classes in S3 are called informal classes, whereas classes in S4 are called formal classes. This chapter covers only S3 classes.

Some Basics on Classes

S3 classes are attributes of S3 objects and are not usually assigned by the user. Given an object, the class of the object can be found by using the function class(). If an object has not been given a class in the package to which the object belongs, then the class of the object is just the mode of the object. For example, an object of mode function is also of class function.

The output from many functions will have a class attribute specific to the function. For example, the class of the output from a linear model fit with the function lm() is lm. Also, objects can belong to more than one class. An example is a model fit using the generalized linear model function glm(). The classes of the output are glm and lm.

On a more technical side, according to the help page for class(), the classes of an object are the classes from which an object inherits. So, the output of lm() inherits from lm and the output from glm() inherits from both lm and glm.

One useful function for classes is the function methods(). Entering **methods(class=*name*)**, where *name* is the name of a class, will show functions specifically written to be applied to objects of the class. For example:

```
> methods(class=matrix)
 [1] anyDuplicated.matrix  as.data.frame.matrix  as.raster.matrix*
 [4] boxplot.matrix        determinant.matrix    duplicated.matrix
 [7] edit.matrix*          head.matrix           isSymmetric.matrix
[10] relist.matrix*        subset.matrix         summary.matrix
[13] tail.matrix           unique.matrix

   Non-visible functions are asterisked
```

Entering **?class** at the R prompt gives more information about classes and inheritance.

Vectors

Although there is no class vector, the vector merits discussion as one of the most basic kinds of objects. For vectors, the class is just the mode of the vector, except for integer vectors, which take on the class integer. Another reason vectors are important is that for the as.name() functions, where *name* is the name of an atomic mode, except for the mode NULL, as.name() returns a vector.

The functions vector(), as.vector(), and is.vector() exist and operate somewhat like the similar functions for the modes. The function vector() takes the arguments **mode** and **length** and creates a vector of the given mode and length. The acceptable modes are the atomic modes—except NULL, the list mode, and the expression mode. Other modes give an error.

For the atomic modes,

```
vector(mode="name", length=n)
```

behaves the same way as

```
name(length=n),
```

where **name** is the name of the mode and **n** is the length argument. Note that **name** must be in quotes in the call to vector(). For the list mode, vector() returns a list of **NULL**s of length given by the length argument. With the mode set equal to **expression**, vector() gives an expression with **NULL**s for arguments, where the number of **NULL**s is given by the length argument.

The function as.vector() tries to coerce an object to a vector. For some objects, as.vector() just passes the object through and does not create a vector. For some other objects, an error is returned if the function as.vector() is run.

For matrices and arrays, dimensional information is removed by as.vector() (for example, names of columns in a matrix and the number of rows and columns), and a vector of the elements of the matrix or array is returned. The elements of the vector are ordered starting with the first dimension of the matrix or array and continuing through the dimensions. For example:

```
> a = array(1:8,c(2,2,2))

> dimnames(a) = list(c("d11","d12"),c("d21","d22"),
+ c("d31","d32"))

> a
, , d31

    d21 d22
d11   1   3
d12   2   4

, , d32
```

```
       d21 d22
d11     5   7
d12     6   8

> as.vector(a)
[1] 1 2 3 4 5 6 7 8
```

Here the c() function is used to create the vector of the dimensions for the 2x2x2 array() and to create names for the three dimensions of the array.

For objects of mode list, as.vector() passes the list through. Depending on the structure of the list, is.vector() operating on the result can give either **TRUE** or **FALSE**. The mode does not change.

For objects of mode function, as.vector() returns an error.

For objects of mode call, as.vector() passes the object through but does not create a vector. The mode does not change.

For objects of mode name, as.vector() returns an error.

For objects of mode expression, as.vector() passes the expression through and the result gives **TRUE** for is.vector(). The mode does not change.

For the S4 mode, as.vector() returns an error.

The function is.vector() returns **TRUE** if the object is a vector and **FALSE** otherwise, although some objects that do not look like vectors return **TRUE**.

More information about vector(), as.vector(), and is.vector() can be found by entering **?vector** at the R prompt.

Some Common Classes

Some common S3 classes are integer, numeric, matrix, and array. Objects of class integer and numeric are vectors. Matrices are just that—objects made up of elements in rows and columns, all of the same mode. Arrays are like matrices, but they can have more than two dimensions.

Some other common S3 classes are ts and mts, for time series; factor, for factors; Date, for dates; and POSIXct, for dates with times, all of which are numeric.

Some common classes of mode list are data.frame, for data frames; POSTXlt, for dates and times; and most output from higher-level functions in the packages such as **lm** and **glm**.

The Matrix Class: matrix

Objects of class matrix are matrices made up of elements of one of the atomic modes, except NULL, or of the modes list or expression. The three functions matrix(), as.matrix(), and is.matrix() exist and behave similarly to the functions for atomic modes.

The function matrix() creates a matrix. The function takes five possible arguments. The first argument is an object of atomic, list, or expression mode. The second argument is **nrow**, the number of rows. The third argument is **ncol**, the number of columns. The fourth argument is **byrow**, which tells R to create the matrix going across rows rather than down columns. The default value is **FALSE**. The **byrow** argument is useful for scanning tabular atomic data into a matrix. The fifth argument is **dimnames**, which assigns names to the rows and columns within the call to matrix(). The default value for **dimnames** is **NULL**.

Using the array **a** from the section on vectors, two examples of creating a matrix follow:

```
> matrix(a,3,3)
     [,1] [,2] [,3]
[1,]   1    4    7
[2,]   2    5    8
[3,]   3    6    1
Warning message:
In matrix(a, 3, 3) :
  data length [8] is not a sub-multiple or multiple of the number of rows [3]
```

and

```
> matrix(a,3,3,byrow=T,dimnames=list(NULL,c("c1","c2","c3")))
     c1 c2 c3
[1,]  1  2  3
[2,]  4  5  6
[3,]  7  8  1
Warning message:
In matrix(a, 3, 3, byrow = T, dimnames = list(NULL, c("c1", "c2",  :
  data length [8] is not a sub-multiple or multiple of the number of rows [3]
```

Note that R gives a warning if the product of the number of rows and columns is not a multiple of the number of elements in the first argument. The warning message does not affect the result.

For the atomic modes, if just the first argument is given, R creates a matrix with the number of rows equal to the number of elements in the object and the number of columns equal to one. If just **nrow** or **ncol** is given, R creates a matrix out of the object in the first argument with the given number of rows or columns, filling out as many of the columns or rows that it takes to use up all of the elements in the first argument—cycling if necessary. If both **nrow** and **ncol** are present, R will go through the elements of the first argument until the matrix is full, cycling as necessary. The **byrow** argument can be used to cycle the first argument across rows rather than down columns.

For objects of the list mode, matrix() creates a matrix that describes the contents of each top level element of the list. The description gives the mode of the element and the size of the element. If the element of the list is not of a legal mode, then a **?** is placed in the cell of the matrix. Referencing cells on the matrix returns the contents of the list for the cell. The following code gives an example:

```
> a.list = list(matrix(1:4,2,2), c("abc","cde"), 1:3, c.fun)

> a.list
[[1]]
```

```
      [,1] [,2]
[1,]    1    3
[2,]    2    4

[[2]]
[1] "abc" "cde"

[[3]]
[1] 1 2 3

[[4]]
function ()
print(1:5)

> matrix(a.list,2,2)
      [,1]        [,2]
[1,] Integer,4    Integer,3
[2,] Character,2  ?

> matrix(a.list,2,2)[2,2]
[[1]]
function ()
print(1:5)
```

Objects of mode expression are legal for matrix(), but the result does look like a matrix. Depending on the number of columns and/or rows given, the arguments in the expression will be duplicated.

The function as.matrix() attempts to coerce an object to class matrix and is mainly used with data.frames. If the argument to as.matrix() can be coerced to a vector and is not a matrix or data.frame, then as.matrix() creates a single column matrix of the coerced elements. The mode is matrix. If the object is a matrix, as.matrix() just returns the matrix and maintains row and column names.

If the object is a data.frame, then as.matrix() coerces the data.frame to a matrix. (A data.frame is a special kind of list for which the elements all have the same length and are of the atomic modes.) If there is a column in the data.frame that contains character data or raw data, then the entire data.frame is coerced to character. Otherwise, the data.frame is coerced to a logical matrix if all of the columns are logical, to an integer matrix if an integer column is present but no numeric or complex columns are present, to a numeric matrix if a numeric column is present and no complex columns are present, and to a complex matrix if a complex column is present.

Data frames can also be converted to a matrix using the data.matrix() function. The function data.matrix() converts a data frame to a matrix by coercing all of the elements in the data frame to numeric. For complex elements, the imaginary part is discarded. The function coerces character columns to NAs and factor columns to integers, starting with 1. (When a data frame is created, columns of mode character are changed to factors by default. See the section on data.frame() for how data.frame() can handle columns of mode character.)

41

The following example shows the results for as.matrix() and data.matrix(), using a data.frame called **a.df**:

```
> a.df = data.frame(c("a","a"),1:2,c(F,T),1:2+.5,1:2+7i)

> dimnames(a.df) = list(c("1","2"),c("char", "int", "log", "doub", "comp"))

> a.df
  char int   log doub comp
1    a   1 FALSE  1.5 1+7i
2    a   2  TRUE  2.5 2+7i

> mode(a.df)
[1] "list"

> class(a.df)
[1] "data.frame"

> as.matrix(a.df)
     char int log     doub  comp
[1,] "a"  "1" "FALSE" "1.5" "1+7i"
[2,] "a"  "2" " TRUE" "2.5" "2+7i"
>
> as.matrix(a.df[,2:5])
     int  log  doub   comp
[1,] 1+0i 0+0i 1.5+0i 1+7i
[2,] 2+0i 1+0i 2.5+0i 2+7i

> class(a.df[,1])
[1] "factor"

> data.matrix(a.df)
     char int log doub comp
[1,]    1   1   0  1.5    1
[2,]    1   2   1  2.5    2
Warning message:
In data.matrix(a.df) : imaginary parts discarded in coercion
```

The function is.matrix() tests whether an object is of class matrix. The function returns **TRUE** if the class of the argument is matrix and **FALSE** otherwise. If an object of mode and class expression is used to create a matrix or is coerced to a matrix, the result will have class matrix, even though the structure of the result is not matrixlike.

More information on matrix(), as.matrix(), and is.matrix() can be found by entering **?matrix** at the R prompt. More information about data.matrix() can be found by entering **?data.matrix** at the R prompt.

The Array Class: array

The array class is a class of data that is organized using dimensions, such as a multidimensional contingency table. Matrices can be set up as two-dimensional arrays and vectors can be set up as one-dimensional arrays. Both, however, will have class matrix, even though array() creates the objects.

The function array() creates an array out of an object. The function takes three arguments. The first argument is any object that can be coerced to a vector. The second argument is a vector that contains the size of each dimension and is of length equal to the number of dimensions. The third argument is a list of names for each of the dimensions and can be omitted. The default value is **NULL**.

The following is an example of setting up an array:

```
> b.array = array(1:12, c(2,3,2),
+ dimnames=list(c("",""),c("d21", "d22", "d23"),NULL))

> b.array
, , 1

  d21 d22 d23
   1   3   5
   2   4   6

, , 2

  d21 d22 d23
   7   9  11
   8  10  12
.
```

Other than there being more than two dimensions, array() behaves the same as matrix().

The function as.array() attempts to coerce an object to class array. The object must be of the atomic modes—except for the NULL mode—or of the list or expression modes. Otherwise, as.array() returns an error. For the atomic modes, as.array() behaves like as.matrix(). For the list and expression modes, as.array() just passes the object through, but changes the class of the object to array. The mode is not changed.

The function is.array() tests an object to see if the class of the object is array. The function returns **TRUE** if the class is array and **FALSE** otherwise.

More information about array(), as.array(), and is.array() can be found by entering **?array** at the R prompt.

The Time Series Classes: ts and mts

Classes ts and mts refer to objects that have a starting point, an end point, and a frequency or period defined, and for which observations are assumed to be at equal intervals. The default time series class for a vector of time series observations is ts. For a matrix of concurrent time series observations, the default classes are mts, ts, and matrix. The class of the time series can be changed when the time series object is created.

Time series objects can be created out of vector, matrix, some list, and expression objects—as well as some other classes of objects such as factor and Date—using the function ts(). Objects of mode array give an error. All of the atomic modes are legal as arguments for the function ts(), except the NULL mode. For list objects, depending on the contents and structure of the list, the ts() function will create a, sometimes strange, time series object.

If the argument to ts() is a data frame, then the data frame is coerced to a matrix by the function data.matrix(). For any object to be used as an argument to ts(), the first element of the object must be atomic. For matrix arguments, the different time series go across the columns and time goes down the rows.

The function ts() takes eight arguments. The first argument is the object to be changed into a time series. The second argument is **start** and gives a value for the start of the series. The third argument is **end** and gives a value for the end of the series. The fourth argument is **frequency**, which give the periodic frequency for the series. The fifth argument is **deltat**, which is the inverse of the frequency. Either **frequency** or **deltat** is supplied, not both.

The sixth argument is **ts.eps**, which gives the acceptable tolerance for comparing frequencies between different time series. The seventh argument is **class**, which tells R what class to assign to the time series object. The eighth argument is **names** and gives names to the time series for time series matrices. If no names are given, R assigns the names **Series 1**, **Series 2**, and so forth.

The second, third, fourth, and fifth arguments can be confusing. R treats monthly or quarterly data as a special case when regarding printing and plotting. Other types of periodic data have to be treated specially. For monthly data, setting **start** equal to

```
start = c('year', 'month number')
```

and frequency equal to

```
frequency = 12
```

or deltat equal to

```
deltat = 1/12,
```

where **year** is the starting year and **month number** is the number of the starting month (**1** for January, **2** for February, and so on), assigns months and years to the points in the object being converted to a time series.

To generate a monthly time series, include **end** with

```
end = c('year', 'month number'),
```

where **year** is the ending year and **month number** is the number of the ending month. The function **ts()** will cycle the first argument until the time series is filled out.

For quarterly data, follow the same steps but use a frequency of four. For example:

```
> d.qua
     [,1] [,2]
[1,] 1.53 5.48
[2,] 7.07 3.51
[3,] 5.91 4.10
[4,] 6.89 8.49
[5,] 1.51 5.33
>
> d.qua.ts = ts(d.qua, start=c(2000, 3), frequency=4)
>
> d.qua.ts
        Series 1 Series 2
2000 Q3    1.53     5.48
2000 Q4    7.07     3.51
2001 Q1    5.91     4.10
2001 Q2    6.89     8.49
2001 Q3    1.51     5.33
```

On a more general level, say there is daily data for one week and three days and the starting week is number 32. Let **d.data** be the data. Then the time series can be created as follows:

```
> d.data
 [1]  0.908 -3.311 -0.702 -0.273  0.574 -0.428 -0.834 -0.531 -3.020 -0.060
>
> d.ts = ts(d.data, start=c(32,1), end=c(33, 3), frequency=7)
>
> d.ts
Time Series:
Start = c(32, 1)
End = c(33, 3)
Frequency = 7
 [1]  0.908 -3.311 -0.702 -0.273  0.574 -0.428 -0.834 -0.531 -3.020 -0.060
>
> print(d.ts, calendar=T)
       p1     p2     p3     p4     p5     p6     p7
32  0.908 -3.311 -0.702 -0.273  0.574 -0.428 -0.834
33 -0.531 -3.020 -0.060
```

Note that the default for printing the time series is not in periods—except for frequencies of 4 and 12, for which R assumes that the data is monthly or quarterly. The printing of periods can be turned on and off with the **calendar** argument to print().

If one number, instead of two, is used for each of **start** and **end**, then only the quantities (n+i/f) can be used as the starting and end points, where **n** is the integer of the first period, **f** is the frequency, and **i** can take integer values between zero and (f-1). The quantity (n+i/f) must be taken out to at least five decimal places if entered manually unless the argument **ts.eps** is changed from the default value of 1.0E-5. The value of **ts.eps** is set in options(). R is very picky here.

The function as.ts() attempts to coerce an object to class ts. Objects that are vector—or matrixlike—will coerce. Arrays will not, functions will not, names will not, and calls will not; expressions and lists will.

The function is.ts() tests if an object is of class ts and returns **TRUE** if so and **FALSE** otherwise.

More information about ts(), as.ts(), and is.ts() can be found by entering **?ts** at the R prompt.

The Factor Classes: factor and ordered

The class factor is the class of objects that are factor levels. Ordered factors belong to two classes, ordered and factor. Ordered factors have ordered factor levels. Factors and ordered factors are used in modeling for which at least some categorical data is present. The mode of factors and ordered factors is numeric and the levels are associated with integers that increase in value from one. However, when printed, the nominal levels are given.

The factor levels are usually ordered alphabetically or numerically by default, depending on the mode of the argument, but the R help page for factor warns that the levels may be sorted by another method.

The three functions factor(), as.factor(), and is.factor() exist, as well as ordered(), as.ordered(), and is.ordered(). The second set of functions behaves the same as the first set with regard to creating and testing factor objects, so we only discuss the first set of functions here.

The function factor() creates a vector of factor levels and an associated list of levels. The function has six arguments. The first argument is the object from which the factors will be generated. The argument must be of an atomic mode other than raw. The second argument is **levels** and sets the order of the factor levels. The **levels** argument is optional.

The third argument is **labels** and assigns labels to the levels. The third argument is optional and defaults to the values of the elements of the object. The fourth argument is **exclude** and gives any levels to be excluded in the result. Excluded levels are set to <NA>. The argument is optional and defaults to **NA**.

The fifth argument is **ordered**, which is in factor(), but not in ordered(). The argument **ordered** tells factor() to create a factor with ordered levels. The function factor() with **ordered** set to **TRUE** gives the same result as the function ordered(). The sixth argument is **nmax** and is described as the maximum number of levels to use. Avoid using **nmax**. The argument does not appear to work and can crash R.

Converting between factors and the original data is sometimes of interest. If labels have not been assigned in factor(),

```
as.mode(levels(fac.obj))[fac.obj],
```

returns the original values of the object, where *mode* is the mode of the original object and **fac.obj** is the factor object. Note that the function,

```
as.numeric(fac.obj),
```

returns the integers associated with the levels, even if the original object was not of mode numeric. If labels have been assigned, then usually the original data cannot be extracted.

An example follows:

```
> a.log = c(T,T,F,T)

> a.log
[1]  TRUE  TRUE FALSE  TRUE

> afl = factor(a.log)

> afl
[1] TRUE  TRUE  FALSE TRUE
Levels: FALSE TRUE

> as.logical(levels(afl))[afl]
[1]  TRUE  TRUE FALSE  TRUE

> as.numeric(afl)
[1] 2 2 1 2

> af2 = factor(a.log, levels=c(T,F))

> af2
[1] TRUE  TRUE  FALSE TRUE
Levels: TRUE FALSE

> as.logical(levels(af2))[af2]
[1]  TRUE  TRUE FALSE  TRUE

> as.numeric(af2)
[1] 1 1 2 1

> af3 =factor(a.log, labels=c("flab","tlab"))

> af3
[1] tlab tlab flab tlab
Levels: flab tlab

> as.logical(levels(af3))[af3]
[1] NA NA NA NA
```

```
> as.numeric(af3)
[1] 2 2 1 2

> as.character(levels(af3))[af3]
[1] "tlab" "tlab" "flab" "tlab"
```

The as.factor() function operates the same way as factor(), but only takes one argument, an object to be made into a factor.

The is.factor() function tests if an object is a factor and returns **TRUE** if so and **FALSE** otherwise.

There is also a related function, addNA(). The function creates a factor object with a level for missing data (NAs). The function takes on two arguments. The first argument is an object from which an object of class factor can be created. The second argument is **ifany**. The **ifany** argument is logical and takes on the value **TRUE** if the extra level is only added when **NA**s are present and the value **FALSE** if the extra level is to always be included.

More information about the seven functions can be found by entering **?factor** at the R prompt.

The Data Frame Class: data.frame

The class data.frame is a matrixlike class of mode list. Data frames and how to use them are important. Many of the data sets that are available for R are data frames. When data is read from external sources, many of the functions that do the reading create data frames. Learning how to work with and create data frames pays high dividends.

Data frames contain atomic data in rows and columns. Within a column, all of the data must be of the same mode. Across columns, the mode can change. Because data frames do not have to be of just one mode, data frames are a special kind of list.

Accessing elements of the data frame can be done like matrices or like lists, which makes data frames more versatile than the usual list. By default, the columns take names that reflect what is or is not in the original objects making up the data frame.

The functions data.frame(), as.data.frame(), and is.data.frame() all exist in R. In data.frame() the objects to be included in the data frame are listed first, separated by commas. The objects can be any object of atomic mode or lists made up of atomic columns, or just raw data. If an object is made up of more than one column, like some matrices and lists, then each column in the original object becomes a column in the data frame. Otherwise, each object becomes a column. If the columns had names in the original objects, the names are brought into the data frame by default.

The objects used to make up the data frame do not have to be of the same length (or number of rows for matrices), but must be multiples of each other in length. The number of rows in the data frame will equal the length of the longest column. The data in the other columns will cycle until the column has the right number of rows. For example:

```
> a.list
[[1]]
```

```
      a1 a2
[1,]   1  7
[2,]   2  8
[3,]   3  9
[4,]   4 10
[5,]   5 11
[6,]   6 12

[[2]]
[1] "abc" "cde"

>
> data.frame(a.list, 1:3)
  a1 a2 c..abc....cde.. X1.3
1  1  7             abc    1
2  2  8             cde    2
3  3  9             abc    3
4  4 10             cde    1
5  5 11             abc    2
6  6 12             cde    3
```

Note that R has created names for the third and fourth columns and that the third and fourth columns both cycle.

The function data.frame() has four arguments in addition to the objects that will make up the data frame. The first argument is **row.names**, which assigns names to the rows and by default is **NULL**, that is, no names are assigned. The second argument is **check.rows**, which is a logical argument and will check for consistency of row lengths and row names if set to **TRUE**. The default is **FALSE**. The third argument is **check.names**, which is also logical and which checks that column names are syntactically correct and corrects names that are not. The default for **check.names** is **TRUE**.

The last argument is **stringsAsFactors**. By default, data.frame() converts any column containing character data into a factor. The argument **stringsAsFactors** is a logical variable. If set to **TRUE**, factors are created. If set to **FALSE**, character columns remain columns of mode character. The actual default value is **default.stingsAsFactors()**. The value of **default.stringsAsFactors()** is set in options() (Chapter 15) and by default is **TRUE** but can be changed in options().

The function I() can be used in the setting up of data frames. The function is another way to stop data.frame() from converting a character vector to factors. Also, I() ensures that for a matrix the column structure is maintained in the data frame. An object in the data.frame() call enclosed in I() will be treated as one element of the data frame, even if the object contains more than one column. Objects enclosed in I() do not cycle. For example:

```
> mat
     one two
row1   1   6
row2   2   7
row3   3   8
row4   4   9
row5   5  10
```

```
> a.char
 [1] "a1"  "a2"  "a3"  "a4"  "a5"  "a6"  "a7"  "a8"  "a9"  "a10"

> data.frame(mat,a.char)
   one two a.char
1   1   6     a1
2   2   7     a2
3   3   8     a3
4   4   9     a4
5   5  10     a5
6   1   6     a6
7   2   7     a7
8   3   8     a8
9   4   9     a9
10  5  10    a10
Warning message:
In data.frame(mat, a.char) :
  row names were found from a short variable and have been discarded

> data.frame(mat,a.char)[[3]]
 [1] a1 a2 a3 a4 a5 a6 a7 a8 a9 a10
Levels: a1 a10 a2 a3 a4 a5 a6 a7 a8 a9
Warning message:
In data.frame(mat, a.char) :
  row names were found from a short variable and have been discarded

> data.frame(I(mat),a.char)
Error in data.frame(I(mat), a.char) :
  arguments imply differing number of rows: 5, 10

> data.frame(I(mat),I(a.char[1:5]))
     mat.one mat.two a.char.1.5.
row1       1       6          a1
row2       2       7          a2
row3       3       8          a3
row4       4       9          a4
row5       5      10          a5

> data.frame(I(mat),I(a.char[1:5]))[[1]]
     one two
row1   1   6
row2   2   7
row3   3   8
row4   4   9
row5   5  10

> data.frame(I(mat),I(a.char[1:5]))[[2]]
[1] "a1" "a2" "a3" "a4" "a5"
```

If row names are not entered in the call to data.frame(), row names are taken from the first column if the first column has row labels and does not cycle. Otherwise, row names are set to **1**, **2**, **3**, and so forth. For example:

```
> z.vec
 istrue isfalse
   TRUE    FALSE
>
> mat[1:4,]
     one two
row1   1   6
row2   2   7
row3   3   8
row4   4   9
>
> y.vec
fac1 fac2 fac3 fac4
"y1" "y2" "y3" "y4"
>
> data.frame(z.vec, mat[1:4,], y.vec)
  z.vec one two y.vec
1  TRUE   1   6    y1
2 FALSE   2   7    y2
3  TRUE   3   8    y3
4 FALSE   4   9    y4
Warning message:
In data.frame(z.vec, mat[1:4, ], y.vec) :
  row names were found from a short variable and have been discarded
>
> data.frame(mat[1:4,], y.vec, z.vec)
     one two y.vec z.vec
row1   1   6    y1  TRUE
row2   2   7    y2 FALSE
row3   3   8    y3  TRUE
row4   4   9    y4 FALSE
```

The function as.data.frame() attempts to coerce an object to a data frame. If the object is a list made up of atomic elements or is an object of an atomic mode, then as.data.frame() creates a data frame out of the object. Otherwise data.frame() gives an error.

The function takes three arguments, **row.names**, **optional**, and **stringsAsFactors**. The arguments **row.names** and **stringsAsFactors** behave the same way as in data.frame(). The argument **optional** is a logical variable that, if set to **TRUE**, tells as.data.frame() that setting row names and converting column names are optional. If set to **TRUE** and if row.names is set to **NULL**, the row names are set to *""*. The default value for **optional** is **FALSE**.

The function is.data.frame() tests if an object is of class data.frame and, if so, returns **TRUE**. Otherwise is.data.frame() returns **FALSE**.

The functions as.matrix() and data.matrix() can be used to convert a data frame to a matrix. See the section on the matrix class for more information about the two kinds of conversions.

For more information about data.frame(), enter **?data.frame** at the R prompt. For more information about as.data.frame() and is.data.frame(), enter **?as.data.frame** at the R prompt. For more information about I(), enter **?I** at the R prompt.

The Date and Time Classes: Date, POSIXct, POSIXlt, and difftime

Sometimes working with dates and times is useful, as when printing and plotting against time. R provides classes for dates and for dates and times. The classes are Date, POSIXct, and POSIXlt. Objects of class Date or POSIXct are of mode numeric and objects of class POSIXlt are of mode list. Of the three types of functions usual for the classes given above, only the functions as.Date(), as.POSIXct(), and as.POSIXlt() exist for date and date and time objects.

To just get a date and time stamp in R, enter **date()** at the R prompt, which returns the day of the week, date, and time. The result is of mode and class character. The system date function Sys.Date() returns the system date and is of numeric mode and class Date. The system date and time function is Sys.time() and returns the system date, time, and time zone and is of mode numeric and classes POSIXct and POSIXlt.

Dates are returned in the format "Year-Month-Day" and times are returned in the format "hour:minute:second." There are a number of functions that operate on the date and time classes, including weekdays(), which returns the day of the week of objects of class Date, POSIXlt, or POSIXlt. More functions can be found at the help page for DateTimeClasses by entering **?DateTimeClasses** at the R prompt.

The function as.Date() creates a date object. The arguments to as.Date() are the object to be converted to a date; **format**, which gives the format of the object in terms of year, month, and day; **origin**, which is an origin for the first argument and must be of class Date or POSIXct; and **tz** for the time zone.

If **origin** is used, the object to be converted can be any numeric object. If **origin** is given, the function adds or subtracts the values of the object to or from the date given by the **origin** argument and converts the result to a date. An example of weekly spacing is

```
> as.Date(0:3*7, "2000-1-1")
[1] "2000-01-01" "2000-01-08" "2000-01-15" "2000-01-22"
.
```

If dates are used as the object and the dates are not in a "year-month-day" format, then the format of the dates must be given. The format is a character variable where the placement of the year is by **%Y**, the day by **%d**, and the month by **%m**, such as

```
> as.Date("1/20/2000", format="%m/%d/%Y")
[1] "2000-01-20"
```

Note that the format is the format of the object to be converted, not the format of the result.

The argument **tz** is for the time zone. Some time zones are recognized, some are not. See the help page for as.Date() for more information.

The function is.Date() tests if an object is a date and returns **TRUE** if so and **FALSE** otherwise.

The functions as.POSIXct() and as.POSIXlt() take the same arguments as Date() except that the dates can contain time, too. The default format for time is **%H:%M:%S** for hours, minutes, and seconds. For example:

```
> as.POSIXct("1/13/2000 00:30:00", format="%m/%d/%Y %H:%M:%S")
[1] "2000-01-13 00:30:00 CST"
```

Dates and dates and times can be operated on by addition and subtraction. Decimals for times are converted correctly. Dates in function Date() are incremented by days; times in the date time functions are incremented by seconds. Examples follow:

```
> as.POSIXct(Sys.time())+1:4*1000
[1] "2014-01-12 15:08:03 CST" "2014-01-12 15:24:43 CST"
[3] "2014-01-12 15:41:23 CST" "2014-01-12 15:58:03 CST"

> mode(as.POSIXct(Sys.time())+1:4*1000)
[1] "numeric"

> as.POSIXlt(Sys.time())+1:4*1000
[1] "2014-01-12 15:08:34 CST" "2014-01-12 15:25:14 CST"
[3] "2014-01-12 15:41:54 CST" "2014-01-12 15:58:34 CST"

> mode(as.POSIXlt(Sys.time())+1:4*1000)
[1] "numeric"

> as.POSIXlt(Sys.time()+1:4*1000)
[1] "2014-01-12 15:09:14 CST" "2014-01-12 15:25:54 CST"
[3] "2014-01-12 15:42:34 CST" "2014-01-12 15:59:14 CST"

> mode(as.POSIXlt(Sys.time()+1:4*1000))
[1] "list"
```

Dates can also be differenced. The class for the difference between dates or dates and times is difftime. The functions difftime() and as.difftime() exist but are not covered here. An example of a date difference is

```
> (Sys.Date()- as.Date("2000-1-1"))
Time difference of 5125 days

> mode(Sys.Date()- as.Date("2000-1-1"))
[1] "numeric"

> class(Sys.Date()- as.Date("2000-1-1"))
[1] "difftime"
```

More information about date and time functions can be found by entering **?Date**, **?as.Date**, **?as.POSIXct**, **?as.POSIXlt**, or **?DateTimeClasses** at the R prompt.

Names for Vectors, Matrices, Arrays, and Lists

A chapter on objects would not be complete without information on how to set names for vectors, matrices, arrays, and lists. Dimension names are always of character mode. For objects of more than one dimension, the name objects are of mode list.

To see what names a vector has or to assign names to a vector, the names() function is used. The function just has one argument, the object. For example:

```
> cde
 [1] 21 22 23 24 25 26 27 28 29 30

> names(cde)
NULL

> names(cde) = paste("v",1:10,sep="")

> cde
 v1  v2  v3  v4  v5  v6  v7  v8  v9 v10
 21  22  23  24  25  26  27  28  29  30

> names(cde)
 [1] "v1"  "v2"  "v3"  "v4"  "v5"  "v6"  "v7"  "v8"  "v9"  "v10"

> mode(names(cde))
[1] "character"

> class(names(cde))
[1] "character"
```

You can also assign names to vectors at the time the vector is created directly. For example:

```
> a.vec = c(a=1,b=2,c=3)
> a.vec
a b c
1 2 3
```

Some objects of mode list are vectors. For such lists, assigning names to the top levels of the list is done with names() or by direct assignment.

For matrices there are three possible functions used to see the names or to assign names: rownames(), colnames(), and dimnames(). The functions rownames() and colnames() have three arguments, the R object, **do.NULL**, and **prefix**. The argument

do.NULL is logical with default value **TRUE**, which tells the function to do nothing if the row or column names are NULL. If **do.NULL** is **FALSE**, the row or column names are indexed with the prefix equal to the value of the argument **prefix**. For example:

```
> mat
     [,1] [,2]
[1,]   1    3
[2,]   2    4

> colnames(mat)
NULL

> colnames(mat) = colnames(mat, do.NULL=F, prefix="cl")

> mat
     cl1 cl2
[1,]   1   3
[2,]   2   4
```

Note that the right-hand side of the third expression only returns the names of the columns and does not do the assignment.

The function dimnames() can be used to assign names to matrices and arrays. If dimnames() operates on an object, then the names of all of the dimensions in the object are returned as a list. If names are assigned using dimnames(), the object on the right side of the assignment must be a list the same number of elements as there are dimensions in the object and with each element either being **NULL** or of the same length as there are elements in each dimension of the matrix or array. For example:

```
> a
, , d31

    d21 d22
d11   1   3
d12   2   4

, , d32

    d21 d22
d11   5   7
d12   6   8

>
> dimnames(a)
[[1]]
[1] "d11" "d12"

[[2]]
[1] "d21" "d22"
```

```
[[3]]
[1] "d31" "d32"

>
> dimnames(a) = list( c("11","12"),c("21","22"),c("31","32") )
>
> a
, , 31

   21 22
11  1  3
12  2  4

, , 32

   21 22
11  5  7
12  6  8

.
```

More information about names can be found by entering **?names**, **?rownames**, or **?dimnames** at the R prompt.

PART 3

■ ■ ■

Functions

Part III covers the basics of functions. Functions are a class of objects that are essentially computer programs. There are tens of thousands of prepackaged functions in R. The user can also develop functions. Chapter 6 describes packaged functions; Chapter 7 shows you how to create new functions; and Chapter 8 explains how to use functions.

When you install R, thirty packages are installed at the same time by default. You can install other packages later. On your computer, packaged functions are stored in packages, which are stored in libraries.

Chapter 6 describes the libraries, lists the packages that are loaded by default when R opens, discusses the primitive functions, gives advice on using help pages, and provides some useful functions related to packages.

Chapter 7 describes the structure of functions. It presents several methods that can be used to create a function and import the function into the R workspace, including the following: using an editor internal to R, inputting the function directly at the console, using an editor external to R with dget( ), and cutting and pasting into R.

Chapter 8 discusses how to call a function, how to use arguments, and what to expect for output.

CHAPTER 6

■ ■ ■

Packaged Functions

R has over 4,800 packages, most of which contain functions. Functions are at the heart of R and provide R with R's great versatility. Functions are R objects, and they are of both mode and class function. Packaged functions are functions that have been created as a part of an R package. On the computer, packages are stored in libraries and are installed to be in a library.

The Libraries

When R is initially installed, currently the packages base, boot, class, cluster, codetools, compiler, datasets, foreign, graphics, grDevices, grid, KernSmooth, lattice, MASS, Matrix, methods, mgcv, nlme, nnet, parallel, rpart, spatial, splines, stats, stats4, survival, tcltk, tools, translations, and utils are also installed in a folder on the hard drive.

To see a listing of the default packages with descriptions of each package and the name of the package folder, enter **library=(lib.loc = .Library)** at the R prompt.

Any packages installed after the initial installation are installed in a different library and are in another folder, which was created when R was installed. Running the function library()with no arguments lists the packages, with descriptions, in the two libraries, separately.

To view all installed packages with much more information about the packages, enter **installed.packages( )**at the R prompt.

Some R functions require other R functions to run. When R is running, only those packages that have been loaded into R from the libraries are accessible to the program. R gives an error if an attempt is made to run a function where a necessary package(s) has not been loaded. Included in the error message are the name(s) of the missing package(s). If a package exists in one of the libraries on the computer, the package can be loaded (made accessible) by entering **library('*package name*')** at the R prompt, where '*package name*' is the name of the package. If the package is not in one of the libraries, installing new packages is straightforward (see Chapter 1). Once installed, the package can be loaded using the library() function. At any given time, entering **search( )**at the R prompt gives a list of the packages that are loaded in the workspace.

To see the functions (and datasets) in a package, enter **library(help='*package name*')** at the R prompt, where '*package name*' is the name of the package. Note that the package must be installed for **library(help='package name')** to return the contents of the package. Some of the files in a package may be datasets, but for most packages the files are generally functions.

Default Packages and Primitive Functions

When a user starts an R session, the packages base, datasets, utils, grDevices, graphics, stats, and methods are the default packages to be loaded into the workspace. (Which default packages are loaded can be changed by changing **defaultPackages** in the function options(). See Chapter 15.) Often, depending on the computing needs of the user, no more packages are needed.

Functions that are written in C and compiled at the time R is compiled are called **primitive** functions. According to the help page found by entering **?primitive** at the R prompt, all primitive functions are in the package base, which is always loaded. The advantage of using primitive functions is that the functions are already compiled, so the functions run faster. The primitive functions include the operators and most of the mathematical functions as well as functions basic to the running and structure of R. A list of the primitive functions can be found at http://cran.r-project.org/doc/manuals/ R-ints.html#g_t_002eInternal-vs-_002ePrimitive. Functions that are not primitive are called **nonprimitive** and are written in R.

Using the Help Pages

Each function in R has a help page, and each help page has essentially the same structure. Like much else in R, the help pages can be daunting at first. However, the help pages often contain a wealth of information.

Given the name of a function, if the package containing the function has been installed, entering **?***function* or **help(***function***)** at the R prompt, where *function* is the name of the function, brings up the help page for the function. Some functions share the same help page. The help page can be brought up using any of the function names.

Title

At the top of a help page is a title that says something about the function(s). For example, for the function lm(), the title is "Fitting Linear Models."

Description

Below the title is a description of how the function(s) is used, headed by the word "Description." The description can be long or short, depending on the complexity of the function(s). For the function lm(), you will find the following description:

```
lm is used to fit linear models. It can be used to carry out regression,
single stratum analysis of variance and analysis of covariance (although aov
may provide a more convenient interface for these).
```

Usage

The section "Usage" is found below the description. In the "Usage" section, the function(s) is listed with all of the possible arguments to the function(s). For arguments with default values, the default values are given.

For the function lm( ), the "Usage" section contains the following:

```
lm(formula, data, subset, weights, na.action, method = "qr",
model = TRUE, x = FALSE, y = FALSE, qr = TRUE,
singular.ok = TRUE, contrasts = NULL, offset, ...)
```

The arguments with default values are the arguments for which the arguments have been set equal to a value.

Arguments

Below the "Usage" section is a section entitled "Arguments." In the "Arguments" section, the arguments found in the "Usage" section are listed with a description of each argument. The description includes the legal values for the argument.

For example, from the lm( ) help page, the first two arguments listed are as follows:

formula	*an object of class "formula" (or one that can be coerced to that class): a symbolic description of the model to be fitted. The details of model specification are given under 'Details'.*
data	*an optional data frame, list or environment (or object coercible by as.data. frame to a data frame) containing the variables in the model. If not found in data, the variables are taken from* environment(formula), *typically the environment from which* lm *is called.*

So, for the function lm( ), the first argument is a formula and the second argument can be a data.frame, but the second argument is optional.

Details

Sometimes there is a section entitled "Details," which gives details related to the arguments. In the lm( ) function example, the section on details gives the rules for setting up a formula and how the function behaves for differing inputs to the formula.

Value

The next section is entitled "Value." The "Value" section gives a description of what is returned from the function(s). For some functions, what functions can operate on the output and what components can be subsetted from the output are relevant and listed in this section.

The first few lines of the "Value" section for the function lm( ) are as follows:

lm *returns an object of class* "lm" *or for multiple responses of class* c("mlm", "lm").

The functions summary *and* anova *are used to obtain and print a summary and analysis of variance table of the results. The generic accessor functions* coefficients, effects, fitted. values, *and* residuals *extract various useful features of the value returned by* lm.

An object of class "lm" is a list containing at least the following components:

coefficients   *a named vector of coefficients*
residuals   *the residuals, that is response minus fitted values. ...*

Some Other Optional Sections

Following the "Value" section, there may be other sections giving more information. For the function lm( ), there are three other sections: "Using time series," "Note," and "Author(s)." Some sections for other functions might be "Warning," "Source," or other headings.

References

The next section is called "References." The "References" section gives references to books and articles related to the method, both for more information and for how the method was derived.

For the function lm( ), the "References" section contains

Chambers, J. M. (1992) Linear models. Chapter 4 of Statistical Models in S eds J. M. Chambers and T. J. Hastie, Wadsworth & Brooks/Cole.

Wilkinson, G. N. and Rogers, C. E. (1973) Symbolic descriptions of factorial models for analysis of variance. Applied Statistics, 22, 392–9.

See Also

The section "See Also" follows the "References" section. The "See Also" section gives information about other functions related to the help page function(s). For the function lm( ), the first three lines of the "See Also" section are the following:

summary.lm *for summaries and* anova.lm *for the ANOVA table;* aov *for a different interface.*

The generic functions coef, effects, residuals, fitted, vcov.

predict.lm *(via* predict) *for prediction, including confidence and prediction intervals;* confint *for confidence intervals of parameters.*

The "See Also" section is a good source for clues to functions related to the method the user is applying.

Examples

The final section, which most pages have, is "Examples." The "Examples" section gives examples of the use of the function(s). Seeing actual examples of usage can be very helpful. From the help page of the function lm( ), part of the example includes the following:

```
require(graphics)

## Annette Dobson (1990) "An Introduction to Generalized Linear Models".
## Page 9: Plant Weight Data.
ctl <- c(4.17,5.58,5.18,6.11,4.50,4.61,5.17,4.53,5.33,5.14)
trt <- c(4.81,4.17,4.41,3.59,5.87,3.83,6.03,4.89,4.32,4.69)
group <- gl(2, 10, 20, labels = c("Ctl","Trt"))
weight <- c(ctl, trt)
lm.D9 <- lm(weight ~ group)
lm.D90 <- lm(weight ~ group - 1) # omitting intercept

anova(lm.D9)
summary(lm.D90)
```

In this example, the structure of a formula is shown rather than explained. Some of the functions that operate on an object of class lm are also shown. Since the package graphics is loaded by default, the call to **require(graphics)** would not normally be necessary.

■ ■ ■

CHAPTER 7

User-Created Functions

User-created functions often make the life of an R user easier. If a repetitive task involves several different lines of code, creating a function to do the task saves time.

Designing plots is one example of when a user-created function makes sense. Plots often take several lines of code, and the design of a plot is usually an interactive process. Creating a function to design the plot is often much easier than using the up arrow and changing lines.

Another example of when a user-created function is useful is when a user wants to try out a statistical technique that is not available in the R packages. Often the user can create a function for the technique using functions that are available.

The Structure of a Function

Nonprimitive functions all have the same structure. On the first line of the function is the word **function**, followed by open and close parentheses, which may or may not contain arguments. In most cases, an open bracket follows the parentheses. Usually, the body of the function is placed below the first line, and the last line is the close bracket. Normally, functions are assigned a name. For example:

```
> d.fun = function( ){
+ print(1:5)
+ }

> d.fun
function( ){
print(1:5)
}

> d.fun( )
[1] 1 2 3 4 5
```

In this example, first, the function is assigned to **d.fun**; next, the content of d.fun( ) is listed; and, last, the function d.fun( ) is run.

The brackets are not necessary if the function consists of just one statement—which can be entered on the same line as the function statement or on the following line(s). For example:

```
> c.fun = function() print(1:5)

> c.fun
function() print(1:5)

> c.fun()
[1] 1 2 3 4 5
```

Again, the function is assigned a name, the function is listed, and the function is run.

Arguments are objects that are used by the function and that must be input to the function at the time the function is run, unless a default value exists for the argument. Arguments are placed within the parentheses when the function is created, separated by commas. A default value is supplied by setting the argument equal to the value. Arguments with default values do not have to be specified when the function is run. If the value is not specified, the function uses the default value.

An example follows of a function with two arguments, where **a** does not have a default value and must be specified, and **b** has the default value of 3:

```
> e.fun = function(a, b=3){
+ print(a:b)
+ }

> e.fun
function(a, b=3){
print(a:b)
}

> e.fun(10)
[1] 10  9  8  7  6  5  4  3

> e.fun()
Error in a:b : 'a' is missing
```

Again, the function is assigned a name, listed, and run. Note that since **a** is the first argument and **b** has a default value, **a** can be supplied without a name. In the second attempt to run e.fun( ), no argument is supplied for **a**, so e.fun( ) returns an error.

Often, the user uses brackets within a function to enclose groups of statements, such as for **if**, **else**, **for**, **while**, and **repeat** groups. There must be the same number of opening brackets as closing brackets in a function; otherwise, the function will not save. Mismatched brackets are a common source of errors in R code.

Lines of code in R (both in a function and at the R prompt) can be broken and continued on the next line. R looks for things such as a closing parenthesis, bracket, or quotation mark to designate the end of a statement or a part of a statement.

Empty lines are legal in R functions. Also, any text can be commented out by placing a pound sign (#) in front of the text. On a line, anything entered after a pound sign is ignored. A piece of advice for writing functions is to write a little chunk at a time, debug at each step, and use plenty of comments.

How to Enter a Function into R

This section describes four ways to get a function into R. The first involves using an editor. The second involves inline entry, as shown in the preceding section. The third involves creating a function outside of R and using dget( ) to get the function into R. The fourth is a variation on the second and third and involves copying and pasting from a source that can be outside of R.

Using an Editor

For the Windows and OS X operating systems, there is a function, edit( ), in the package utils that works well for creating new functions. The purpose of the function edit( ) is to call an editing function.

In Windows, the default editing function is the **internal** editor. The possible other choices for editor are xedit( ), emacs( ), xemacs( ), vi( ), and pica( ), where the choice is available only if the editor is present on the system. The default editor is listed in options( ) and can be changed at any time (Chapter 15).

For OS X systems, the only editor available is the **vi** editor, which works well.

For Linux operating systems, calling edit( ) from the terminal window does not give a good result. A better editor is emacs( ), which is available for Linux systems.

Most of the preceding information is from the help page for edit( ). Enter **?edit** at the R prompt for more information about the editing functions.

To create an object that is a function by using an editor, the function is first assigned to a name. For example, let the name be **f.fun**. To create the function **f.fun( )**, start by entering **f.fun = function( ){}** at the R prompt. The object f.fun then contains a function with no arguments and no statements.

The next step is to edit the function. For simplicity, only the function edit( ) is shown in the example here. The other editors behave similarly. Enter **f.fun = edit(f.fun)** at the R prompt. An editing window opens up for editing (Figure 7-1).

```
R                            R Console
> f.fun = function(){}
>
> f.fun = edit(f.fun)
```

```
R                                    f.fun - R Editor
function(){}
```

Figure 7-1. *Creating a function: the first and second steps*

For the third step, the arguments are entered within the parentheses and the statements of the function are entered within the brackets (Figure 7-2).

```
R                            R Console
> f.fun = function(){}
>
> f.fun = edit(f.fun)
```

```
R                                    f.fun - R Editor
function(mu, se=1, alpha=.05){
    z_value = qnorm(1-alpha/2, mu, se)
    print(z_value)
}
```

Figure 7-2. *Creating a function: the third step*

The fourth step is to exit the editor. To exit the editor, click the **x** at the top right-hand corner of the editing window. A window will appear with options to save the file, exit without saving, or to cancel the request and go back to editing. (If no changes were made to the file, the options screen does not appear.) Click **Yes** to save the changes, **No** to revert to the earlier version, or **Cancel** to go back to editing.

If the function is syntactically correct, the function will save. Otherwise, edit( ) returns an error, such as the following:

```
Error in .External2(C_edit, name, file, title, editor) :
  unexpected '}' occurred on line 4
 use a command like
 x <- edit()
 to recover
```

To recover the work already done, enter **f.fun = edit( )**. Using parentheses with no content is very important. If the name of the function is entered within the parentheses, the editing changes are lost and the function reverts to the version before the edit. Note that the error message gives information about the problem with the R code.

The following shows the input and output at the R console when creating the function f.fun( ) with the editor, followed by the listing of the function, and the running of the function with the first argument set to zero.

```
> f.fun = function( ){}

> f.fun = edit(f.fun)

> f.fun
function(mu, se=1, alpha=.05){
  z_value = qnorm(1-alpha/2, mu, se)
  print(z_value)
}

> f.fun(0)
[1] 1.959964.
```

Inline Entry

As shown in the first section of this chapter, a function can be entered inline. Let b.fun be the name of a new function created to list the digits three through six. Then the steps to create the function, to list the code, and to run the function are as follows:

```
> b.fun = function( ){
+ print(3:6)
+ }

> b.fun
function( ){
print(3:6)
}

> b.fun()
[1] 3 4 5 6
```

If a syntactical error is made in the process of entering a function inline, R will give an error and return to the R prompt. For example:

```
> b.fun = function( ){
+ print(3:6
+ }
Error: unexpected '}' in:
"print(3:6
}"
```

For longer functions, using the R editor or an external editor tends to be less frustrating.

An Outside Editor: dget( ) and Copying and Pasting

An outside editor can be used to create a function. Any editor that produces text files, such as **Notepad**, **TextEdit**, or **gedit**, can be used to create an R function. The rules for creating a function are the same as those described in the first section. Once the function is created, the function can be imported into the workspace by using the function dget( ) or by copying and pasting. (The function dget( ) and the corresponding function dput( ) are one way to import and export functions in R.)

Say that a function is in a file called **function.txt** in the same folder as the R workspace and that the function is syntactically correct. Then the following line imports the function into the object g.fun:

```
g.fun = dget("function.txt")
```

(Note that R accepts more complex file paths for files, including absolute addresses on the hard drive and URLs.)

If the text file is not syntactically correct, R returns an error with information about the syntactical problem in the file.

The file can also be copied and pasted from an outside source—or from elsewhere in the R session—into an object in R. Start by copying the function onto the clipboard of the computer. Next, enter the name that the object is to be called, followed by an equal sign, at the R prompt. The cursor should then be to the right of the equal sign. Next, paste.

If the function is syntactically correct, the cursor stops to the right of the close bracket. Press the **Return** key to complete the process. If the function is not syntactically correct, copying and pasting will give an error containing information about the problem with the syntax.

CHAPTER 8

How to Use a Function

Most functions require specific kinds of arguments, which must be input into the function correctly. For example, if a function calls for a matrix and a data.frame is input, the function will return an error. Since external tables are often read into the R workspace as data.frames, using a data.frame for a matrix is quite a common error. This chapter covers calling a function, using arguments, and accessing output.

Calling a Function

Calling a function is straightforward. The name of the function is entered at the R prompt followed by a set of parentheses which may or may not contain arguments, depending on the function. If the function does require arguments, the arguments are separated by commas within the parentheses.

Sometimes the argument name must be used, but not always. For values that are entered without names, R assigns the values to the arguments which are unnamed in the call, starting with the first unnamed variable and continuing in order until the unnamed arguments are exhausted. The order of the arguments is the order of the arguments within the parentheses of the function definition.

To illustrate the use of arguments, an example follows using a function named f.fun(). The function f.fun() calculates a quantile of the normal distribution given the mean, the standard deviation, and alpha. The function returns the (1-alpha/2) x 100th percentile of the distribution. The arguments 'se' and 'alpha' are given default values and 'mu' is not.

The example starts with a definition of the function, which is followed by five different calls to the function:

```
> f.fun = function(mu, se=1, alpha=.05){
  q_value = qnorm(1-alpha/2, mu, se)
  print(q_value)
}

> f.fun(mu=0, se=1, alpha=0.05)
[1] 1.959964
```

In the first call, each of the arguments are specified by name. In R, arguments can be in any order if specified by name.

```
> f.fun(0,1,0.10)
[1] 1.644854
```

In the second call, the values for the arguments are entered without names. Since the arguments are entered in order, the function knows which argument to assign to which value. The argument 'mu' takes on the value of '0', 'se' the value of '1', and 'alpha' the value of '0.10', which is the order of the arguments within the parentheses in the function.

```
> f.fun(0, alpha=0.20)
[1] 1.281552
```

In the third call, the first argument is entered without a name and the third argument is entered with a name. The second argument takes on the default value. The argument 'mu' takes on the value of '0', 'se' the value of '1', and 'alpha' the value of '0.20'.

```
> f.fun(4, 4)
[1] 11.83986
```

In the fourth call, values for the first two arguments are entered without names and the third argument takes on the default value. The argument 'mu' takes on the value of '4', as does 'se'. The argument 'alpha' takes on the default value of '0.05'.

```
> f.fun( se=1, 0, 0.2)
[1] 1.281552
```

In the fifth call, the second argument is named and the first and third are not, so 'mu' takes on the value '0' and 'alpha' takes on the value '0.2', while 'se' takes on the value '1'. Note that the named argument can be placed anywhere in the list.

Arguments

Given a function, a listing of the arguments to the function can be found at the help page for the function. For some functions, the user must know something about the theory behind the function to understand the arguments, but for many functions the arguments are straightforward. As noted in the last section, arguments with default values do not have to be given a value when the function is called.

Arguments to a function must be of the correct mode and class. On the help page of a function, descriptions of the arguments are listed in the 'Arguments' section, sometimes giving the mode and(or) class, but not always. Sometimes the mode and(or) class is obvious. Sometimes more information can be found in the 'Details' section. Sometimes looking in the 'Examples' section is enough to clear up the form of an argument.

One argument which needs a little explaining is the "..." argument. The "..." argument tells the user that there are more arguments that may be entered. The arguments would be to a lower-level function called by the higher-level function. An example follows.

The example starts by listing two vectors, 'x' and 'y', and then continues with two calls to the function lm() with two different values for the argument 'tol'. (The function lm() fits a linear model.) On the help page for lm() there is no argument 'tol'. However there is the argument "..", indicating that lm() calls another function for which an argument can be entered.

The function lm.fit() is a lower level function which lm() calls and lm.fit() has the argument 'tol'. (The argument 'tol' gives the tolerance for the QR decomposition as to whether a matrix is singular.) In the first call to lm() the default value for 'tol' is used, since 'tol' is not specified. In the second call, lm() passes the value for 'tol' to lm.fit().

```
> x
[1] 2.001 2.000 2.000

> y
[1] 4.03 4.00 4.01

> lm(y~x)

Call:
lm(formula = y ~ x)

Coefficients:
(Intercept)            x
     -45.99        25.00

> lm(y~x, tol=.001)

Call:
lm(formula = y ~ x, tol = 0.001)

Coefficients:
(Intercept)            x
      4.013           NA
```

In the first call, the default value for 'tol' is 1.0e-7, so lm.fit() does not find a linear dependency in the matrix consisting of a column of ones and 'x'. As a result two coefficients are fit.

In the second call, 'tol' is set to 1.0e-3 and lm() determines that there is a linear dependency in the matrix consisting of a column of ones and 'x', so only one coefficient is fit.

The Output from a Function

The output from a function will vary with the function. Plotting functions mainly give plots. Summary functions give summarized results. Functions that test a hypothesis give the results from the test.

Most packaged functions print some results directly to the screen, but most packaged functions also have output which can be accessed through subscripting. For example, looking at the help page of the function lm(), under the 'Value' Section, coefficients, residuals, fitted.values, rank, weights, df.residual, call, terms, contrasts, xlevels, offset, y, x, model, and na.action are all values which can be accessed from a call to the function.

The most common method used to access values is with the '$' operator, although index subscripting can be used too. For most functions the output is of mode list. The elements of the list can be of any mode.

For the first simple regression model fit in the last section, the accessible fifteen values are as follows:

```
> a.lm = lm(y~x)

> a.lm$coef
(Intercept)            x
   -45.995       25.000

> a.lm$res
            1             2            3
-4.336809e-19 -5.000000e-03  5.000000e-03

> a.lm$fit
    1     2     3
4.030 4.005 4.005

> a.lm$rank
[1] 2

> a.lm$weights
NULL

> a.lm$df
[1] 1

> a.lm$call
lm(formula = y ~ x)

> a.lm$terms
y ~ x
attr(,"variables")
list(y, x)
attr(,"factors")
  x
y 0
x 1
attr(,"term.labels")
[1] "x"
```

```
attr(,"order")
[1] 1
attr(,"intercept")
[1] 1
attr(,"response")
[1] 1
attr(,".Environment")
<environment: R_GlobalEnv>
attr(,"predvars")
list(y, x)
attr(,"dataClasses")
        y         x
"numeric" "numeric"

> a.lm$contrasts
NULL

> a.lm$xlevels
named list()

> a.lm$offset
NULL

> a.lm$y
NULL

> a.lm$x
named list()

> a.lm$model
     y      x
1 4.03 2.001
2 4.00 2.000
3 4.01 2.000

> a.lm$na.action
NULL
```

In the example, the call to lm() was assigned a name, but lm() could have been subscripted directly. An example is lm(y~x)$coef. Values accessed from a call to a function are often used in another function.

Running an R function takes a little care, but with some experimentation and determination, the results can be very useful.

PART 4

Inputting and Creating Data, Outputting Data and Output, and Manipulating Objects

Part IV covers importing data from external sources, creating new data, exporting data and the output from functions, and manipulating some common kinds of objects.

Chapter 9 introduces some functions used to import data, some functions used to create data, and some probability distributions, from which random numbers can be generated.

Chapter 10 gives some ways to export from R. Each method is specific to the kind of object to be exported.

Chapter 11 concerns manipulating objects.

■ ■ ■

Importing and Creating Data

When you are loading data into R, you have a number of options. For external files, there are several functions that read specific kinds of files or data. R also comes with a number of data sets that can be loaded. Sometimes the user wants to create data. R has a multitude of random number generators for data creation. Data can be entered manually using c() or by using various other functions to create data with certain patterns.

The first section of this chapter covers reading data into R and loading R data sets. The second section covers probability distributions, including random number generators and the function sample(). The third section covers manual data entry and creating data with patterns.

Reading Data into R, Including R Data Sets

There are a number of R functions that read data into R. The most common ones are scan() to read data of a given mode, and read.table() and read.csv() to read data from a matrix structured table. Some of the more exotic ones are read.fortran() to read data coded in FORTRAN format, read.fwf() for reading tables in fixed width format, read.xls() for Excel spreadsheets (the creators of R recommend against reading a Excel file directly but provide some functions to do so), and read.delim() for tab delineated columns. For a complete listing, see http://cran.r-project.org/doc/manuals/r-release/R-data.html.

The Function scan()

The function scan() imports data from a file row-by-row, either from the values to the argument **text** or directly from the console. For importing a file, the rows do not have to be of the same length. The function reads data of the modes logical, numeric, complex, character, raw, and list. For all of the modes except list, all of the data must be readable as the mode.

The function scan() is most often used to read an external file. The reference to the file comes first in the call and must be contained within quotes. The reference may be relative to the location of the workspace or an absolute location—including URLs. An example is

```
> scan("test.txt")
Read 7 items
[1] 1 3 5 7 1 4 6
```

where test.txt is a file containing the seven digits in two rows. To browse for a file, enter **file.choose()** for the quoted file reference, that is **scan(file.choose())**.

The function can also be used to read in data at the console, which is done by setting the data equal to an argument called **text**, where the data is in quotation marks. For example:

```
> scan(text = "1 2 3 4")
Read 4 items
[1] 1 2 3 4
```

Data can also be read in directly from the console by setting the file equal to " ". For example:

```
> scan("")
1: 1
2: 4
3: 9
4: 3
5:
Read 4 items
[1] 1 4 9 3
```

Here R cues for a data point with the point number followed by a colon. To stop entering data, use **control-z** in Windows and **control-d** in Linux, or enter a blank line by pressing the **return(enter)** key.

If the mode of the data being entered is not numeric, the argument **what** must be included in the call to scan(). The argument **what** is set equal to mode(), where *mode* is the mode of the data. For example:

```
> scan("test.txt", what=complex())
Read 7 items
[1] 1+0i 3+0i 5+0i 7+0i 1+0i 4+0i 6+0i
```

which reads complex data from the external file test.txt. If the data in the file is not readable as the mode, scan() returns an error.

The function scan() also has the argument **sep**, which tells scan() the separator between values in either an external file or in the value of **text**. By default, the separator is white space. The argument **sep** can be set to any one-byte value that R can read. In the call to scan(), the value for **sep** is placed within quotation marks. For example:

```
> scan(text = "1, 2, 3, 4", sep=",")
Read 4 items
[1] 1 2 3 4
```

Here a comma is used as the separator between data values.

If two separating symbols in the call to scan() do not have a value between the two, then by default the value is set to **NA**. For example:

```
> scan(text = "1, 2, 3,, 4", sep=",")
Read 5 items
[1]  1  2  3 NA  4
```

For data with header lines, the argument **skip** tells scan() to skip lines before reading data. The value of **skip** tells scan() how many lines to skip and can be of any atomic mode. The value is coerced to an integer if possible or else interpreted as zero. If **skip** equals zero, no lines are skipped.

To read a header line, the argument **nlines** tells scan() to read lines up to and including the value of **nlines**. Like **skip**, **nlines** can be of any atomic mode and scan() coerces the value to integer. If nlines is set to zero, all lines are read.

The function scan() returns a vector. To create a matrix or array, the call to scan() can be part of a call to matrix() or array(). For example:

```
> matrix(scan( text="1 2 3 4 5 6 7 8 9 10" ), 2, 5, byrow=T)
Read 10 items
     [,1] [,2] [,3] [,4] [,5]
[1,]    1    2    3    4    5
[2,]    6    7    8    9   10
```

There are several other arguments for scan() that do things such as limit the number of data points to be read, fill out lines of incomplete data, or tell scan() the style of the decimal point in the data. More information can be found by entering **?scan** at the R prompt.

The Functions read.table(), read.csv(), and read.delim()

The three functions read.table(), read.csv(), and read.delim() are essentially the same function, differing only in the default values of the argument **sep** and the argument **header**. As with the function scan(), the argument **sep** gives the symbol used to separate values of the data in the file and can be any one byte value. The argument **header** takes on logical values and tells the function whether to read a header from the first line or not.

The three functions import data from a file, where the file is in the form of a matrix, or from values of the argument **text**. If the data is from a file, the location of the file is entered first in the call within quotation marks. The location of the file can be relative to the workspace or absolute, including URLs. To browse for a file, enter **file.choose()** for the quoted name, for example, **read.table(file.choose())**. An example with a quoted name follows:

```
> read.table("test2.txt")
   V1 V2 V3 V4
1 one  3  5  7
2 two  4  6  8
```

Note that the columns do not have to be of the same mode. Here the file `test2.txt` contains both character and numeric data and is in the same folder as the R workspace.

If the rows in the file are not all of the same length, by default the function will return an error. The argument **fill** is a logical argument and tells R to fill out rows that have fewer elements than other rows. For example:

```
> read.table("test4.txt", fill=T)
  V1 V2 V3 V4
1 one  3  5  7
2 two  4  6 NA
```

Here `test4.txt` is missing the last element of the second row. R fills in the element with **NA**.

If the argument **text** is used to enter a table, the end of a row is indicated by \n. For example:

```
> read.table(text="1 2 3 4 \n 2 3 4 5")
  V1 V2 V3 V4
1  1  2  3  4
2  2  3  4  5
```

For `read.table()`, the default value for **sep** is white space and the default value for **header** is **FALSE**. For `read.csv()`, the default value for **sep** is a comma and the default value for **header** is **TRUE**. For `read.delim()`, the default value for **sep** is a tab—which in R is entered as \t—and the default value for **header** is **TRUE**. (There are two other related functions, `read.csv2()` and `read.delim2()`, which are for European use and have **dec**, the style of the decimal point, set equal to ',', and, for `read.csv2()`, **sep** set equal to ;.)

The three functions create a data.frame out of the data, so the modes of the elements only need to be consistent down the columns. If a column contains character data, then by default the column is converted to a factor. By setting the argument **as.is** to **TRUE**, the conversion is to character. For example:

```
> read.table("test3.txt", sep=",")
   V1    V2 V3 V4
1 one     1  3  4
2   1  four  3  2
```

```
> class(read.table("test3.txt", sep=",")[,1])
[1] "factor"
```

```
> class(read.table("test3.txt", sep=",")[,3])
[1] "integer"
```

```
> read.table("test3.txt", sep=",", as.is=T)
   V1    V2 V3 V4
1 one     1  3  4
2   1  four  3  2
```

```
> class(read.table("test.txt3", sep=",", as.is=T)[,1])
[1] "character"
```

```
> class(read.table("test.txt3", sep=",", as.is=T)[,3])
[1] "integer"
```

You can see the difference between not setting **as.is** and setting **as.is** to **TRUE**. The file test3.txt is a file in the same folder as the workspace, is in matrix form, and contains both character and integer data.

The three functions can read some types of atomic data: logical, numeric, complex, and character. From the R help page for the three functions, R reads in the data as character data and then converts from character to one of the classes logical, integer, numeric, complex, or factor.

As noted above, if **as.is** is set to **TRUE**, columns containing character data are not converted to factors but retain the class character. The argument **as.is** can also be entered as a logical vector with a value for each column. A shorter vector can be entered also, with the values cycling across the columns.

The argument **colClasses** manually sets the class of each column and can be used in place of **as.is** to keep a column in character mode. The possible values for the column classes are NA, NULL, logical, integer, numeric, complex, raw, character, factor, Date or POSIXct. The values are quoted, except for **NA** and **NULL**, and are entered as a vector. The values will cycle.

If the value is **NA**, the normal conversion will take place. Otherwise, if possible, the column elements are coerced to the class listed for the column. For example:

```
> read.table("test2.txt", colClasses=c("character","factor",NA,NA))
  V1 V2 V3 V4
1 one  3  5  7
2 two  4  6  8
```

```
> class(read.table("test2.txt", colClasses=c("character","factor",NA,NA))
[,1])
[1] "character"
```

```
> class(read.table("test2.txt", colClasses=c("character","factor",NA,NA))
[,2])
[1] "factor"
```

```
> class(read.table("test2.txt", colClasses=c("character","factor",NA,NA))
[,3])
[1] "integer"
```

The arguments **row.names** and **col.names** are used to give names to the rows and columns of the data.frame. For **row.names**, the argument can be a character vector of length equal to the number of rows in the data.frame; the argument can be an integer specifying which column in the data.frame to use as row names; or the argument can be a character value containing the name of the column to be used as the row names. The row names do not cycle.

For **col.names**, the argument is a character vector of names for the columns. The vector must be of the same length as the number of columns. If **col.names** is not specified and **header** is **FALSE**, then the columns are named V1, V2,…, Vn, where **n** is the number of the last column.

If **header** is **TRUE** and the first column does not have a name, while the rest of the columns do, then R sets the first column as the row names.

Some examples are the following:

For the matrix

$$\begin{bmatrix} & \text{"c1"} & \text{"c2"} & \text{c3} \\ \text{"one"} & 3 & 5 & 7 \\ \text{"two"} & 4 & 6 & 8 \end{bmatrix}$$

which is the file test5.txt, the example is

```
> read.table("test5.txt", header=T)
    c1 c2 c3
one  3  5  7
two  4  6  8
```

Note that **header** is **TRUE**, and there is one less row in the first column.

For a matrix consisting of the second two rows of test5.txt, called test6.txt, an example follows:

```
> read.table("test6.txt", col.names=c("c1","c2","c3","c4"), row.names=2)
  c1 c3 c4
3 one  5  7
4 two  6  8
```

The four names are assigned to the four columns and then column two is used for the names of the rows while the other columns retain the assigned names.

There are several other arguments for the functions read.table(), read.csv(), and read.delim(). A full description of the functions can be found by entering **?read.table** at the R prompt.

R Data Sets

R comes with a number of data sets. Some of these data sets are found in the package **datasets**, which is one of the packages installed by default in R. To load data sets from the package **datasets**, enter **library(datasets)** at the R prompt. To see the data sets in **datasets**, enter **library(help=datasets)** at the R prompt. Once the library is loaded, the data sets in **datasets** are accessible by entering the name of the data set.

For any library, once the library is loaded, the data sets in the library are accessible like any other object in the workspace. The packaged data sets are not necessarily data. frames, but many are.

Other Functions to Import Files

Other functions for importing files will not be covered here. A search on **read**, done by entering **??read** at the R prompt, gives many of the functions that read into the R workspace.

For Excel spreadsheets, the R writers recommend exporting an Excel spreadsheet to a .csv (comma separated values) file and reading the .csv file into R. There are a few functions to read Excel spreadsheets, but the R writers say the conversion is full of pitfalls.

Probability Distributions and the Function sample()

R has a wealth of random number generators. The random number generators are one of four functions associated with the probability distributions, all of which are covered here. The functions associated with probability distributions mostly have the same form. Many of the distributions can be found by entering **??distributions** at the R prompt. Entering **?distribution** at the R prompt gives the distributions—and generators—in the package **stats**.

Probability Distributions

For the probability distributions in the package **stats**, there are four functions associated with a distribution: ddist(), pdist(), qdist(), and rdist(), where *dist* describes the distribution. For example, for the normal distribution, *dist* equals **norm**. Not all distributions have all four.

The first function is the function for the density. The function, ddist(), gives the heights of the probability density function at specified values of a vector of numbers. The second function is for the cumulative probability. The function, pdist(), by default gives the areas under the probability density function to the left of the specified values of a vector of numbers.

The third function is for quantiles. The function, qdist(), by default gives the values on the real line for which the areas to the left of the values are equal to the values of a specified vector of probabilities. The fourth function is the random number generator. The function, r*dist*(), generates pseudorandom variables from the distribution. For all of the functions, the vectors can be vectors of length one.

The four functions have arguments to specify the standard parameters of the given distribution, for many of which there are defaults. For example, for the normal distribution the arguments are **mean** and **sd** and are set equal to **0** and **1** by default. Both the variables **mean** and **sd** can be entered as vectors and will cycle. The vectors must be numeric or logical. Logical vectors are coerced to numeric. The distributions in the package stats are given in Table 9-1 along with the parameter arguments for the distributions.

Table 9-1. *Probability Distributions in Package* **Stats**

Distribution Name in R	Parameters of the Distribution
beta	shape1=1, shape2=2, npc=0
binom	size, prob
birthday	classes=365, coincident=2
cauchy	location=0, scale=1
chisq	df, npc=0
exp	rate=1
f	df1, df2, npc
gamma	shape, rate=1, scale=1/rate
geom	prob
hyper	m, n, k
lnorm	meanlog=0, sdlog=1
multinom	size, prob
nbinom	size, prob, mu
norm	mean=0, sd=1
pois	lambda
signrank	n
t	df, ncp
tukey	nmeans, df, nranges=1
unif	min=0, max=1
weibull	shape, scale=1
wilcox	m, n

The prefixes are d, p, q, r. The multinom function only has d and r. The tukey function only has p and q. The birthday function only has p and q and does not have a **log.p** *argument. From the CRAN help page for distribution.*

For all of the four functions, the first argument is required and does not have a default. For the density functions, the first argument **x** is a vector of real numbers or values that can be coerced to real numbers. For the cumulative probability functions, the first argument **q** is also a vector of real numbers or values that can be coerced to real numbers. For the quantile functions, the first argument **p** is a vector of probabilities or values that can be coerced to a value between zero and one inclusive. For the random number generators, the first argument **n** (**nn** for the hypergeometric, sign rank, and wilcox distributions) is a positive integer, or a value that can be coerced to integer, that tells R how many numbers to generate.

In general, for the density functions, if the values of the first argument are to be considered as logs of the values of interest, the logical argument **log** is set to **TRUE**. For the probability and quantile functions, the logical argument **log.p** is set to true if the values that are for the probabilities are entered or output as logs of the probabilities.

In general, for the cumulative probability and quantile functions, whether to use the upper tail or the lower tail of the distribution can be set using the logical argument **lower.tail**. The lower tail is set by default. Lower tails are the area under the distribution function for values less than or equal to the values of the first argument, and upper tails are the area under the distribution function for values greater than the values of the first argument.

Also, in general, parameters can be entered as vectors and will cycle. If an illegal value for a parameter is entered, the function will give an error.

More information about a given probability distribution can be found by entering **?ddist** at the R prompt, where *dist* is the name of the distribution from Table 9-1, except for the tukey and birthday distributions for which **?pdist** works.

The Function sample()

Sometimes a random sample is needed rather than random numbers. The function sample() takes a random sample of atomic objects, list objects, or any other mode object for which length is defined.

The function sample() takes four arguments. The first argument, **x**, is the object to be sampled. If **x** is a single positive real number greater than one, sample() samples from the sequence from 1 to the real number rounded down to an integer. If **x** is an object that can be coerced to a vector or a single positive number and no other arguments are given, sample() returns a permutation of the object or the sequence from one to the number rounded down to an integer.

The second argument **size** is the number of items to be sampled. The argument **size** can be a nonnegative integer or a real number that can be rounded down to a nonnegative integer.

The third argument is the logical argument **replace**, which tells sample() whether to sample with replacement. The default value is **FALSE**, that is to sample without replacement. If **size** is larger than the length of **x** and **replace** is **FALSE**, then sample() will give an error.

The fourth argument is **prob** and gives a list of weights for the sampling. The argument **prob** must be of the same length as **x**, must have elements that can be coerced to non-negative numeric elements and for which at least half of the coerced elements are nonzero. The coerced elements of **prob** do not have to sum to one.

For example:

```
> sample(10)
 [1]  8 10  6  4  7  5  3  9  1  2

> sample(10, 5)
 [1] 3 1 6 8 9

> sample(c("a1", "a2", "a3"), 6, replace=T)
 [1] "a1" "a1" "a1" "a3" "a3" "a1"

> sample(11:21, prob=1:11)
 [1] 18 20 14 21 19 17 12 16 15 13 11
```

More information about sample() can be found by entering **?sample** at the R prompt.

Manually Entering Data and Generating Data with Patterns

Data can be entered manually using the function c(), where the **c** stands for *collect*. Sometimes data with a certain pattern is needed, for example, in setting up indices for matrix or array manipulation or as input to functions. There are a number of functions in R that give patterned results, which can be useful. Sometimes indexed names are needed for dimensions in a vector, matrix, or array. The function paste() can be used to create indexed names.

The Function c()

The function c() collects objects together into a single object. The objects to be collected are separated by commas within the call to c(). The objects can be NULL, raw, logical, integer, double, character strings (which must be quoted), named objects (which must be atomic objects, lists, or expressions), lists, and/or expressions. Objects can also be functional calls that return any of the above classes.

If all of the objects in the call are atomic objects, the function c() collects the objects into a vector of the elements making up the objects. The class of the resulting vector is the highest level class within the elements of the vector, where the levels of the classes increase in the order NULL, raw, logical, integer, double, complex, and character.

An example of the hierarchy follows:

```
> rw = as.raw(c(36, 37, 38, 39))

> rw
[1] 24 25 26 27

> c(rw, rw)
[1] 24 25 26 27 24 25 26 27
```

```
> c(rw, TRUE)
[1] TRUE TRUE TRUE TRUE TRUE

> c(rw, 40)
[1] 36 37 38 39 40

> c(rw, 40.5)
[1] 36.0 37.0 38.0 39.0 40.5

> c(rw, 1+1i)
[1] 36+0i 37+0i 38+0i 39+0i  1+1i

> c(rw, "six")
[1] "24" "25" "26" "27" "six"
```

The conversion from raw is automatic except for the conversion to character, which maintains the raw values.

The function c() has one possible named argument, the logical argument **recursive**. The default value of **recursive** is **FALSE**. If **recursive** is set to **TRUE** and the collection contains a list but not an expression, then the list is taken apart to the lowest level of the individual elements in the list and a vector of atomic elements is returned. The object takes on the class of the highest level of class in the object. If **recursive** is **FALSE**, the resulting object becomes a list.

In the hierarchy of classes, list is above the atomic classes but below expression. If an expression is included in the call to c(), then the result has class expression.

An example for objects of class list and expression follows:

```
> a.list
[[1]]
     cl1 cl2
[1,]   1   3
[2,]   2   4

[[2]]
[1] "abc" "cde"

> c(a.list, 1:2)
[[1]]
     cl1 cl2
[1,]   1   3
[2,]   2   4

[[2]]
[1] "abc" "cde"

[[3]]
[1] 1

[[4]]
[1] 2
```

```
> c(a.list, 1:2, recursive=T)
[1] "1"   "2"   "3"   "4"   "abc" "cde" "1"   "2"
```

```
> a.expr = expression(y ~ x, `1`)
```

```
> c(a.list, a.expr)
expression(1:4, c("abc", "cde"), y ~ x, `1`)
```

In the first call to c(), an object of class list is returned. In the second call, an object of class character is returned. In the third call, an object of class expression is returned.

Names can be assigned to the elements of the object created by c() by setting the elements equal to a name in the listing—for example:

```
> c(a=1,b=2,3)
a b
1 2 3
```

Here the first two elements are assigned the names a and b while the third element is not assigned a name.

More information about c() can be found by entering ?c at the R prompt.

The Functions seq() and rep()

The functions seq() and rep() are used for sequences and repeated patterns. In the simplest form, using seq() is the same as using the colon operator to create a sequence. However, seq() can create more sophisticated sequences than the colon operator. The function rep() repeats the first argument to the function a specified number of times, where there are two possible ways to do the repetition.

The Function seq()

The function seq() has six arguments. The first two arguments are the starting and ending values of the sequence and are named **from** and **to**. The arguments **from** and **to** can take on logical, numeric, or complex values. For logical values, **TRUE** is coerced to one and **FALSE** is coerced to zero. For complex values, the imaginary part is dropped. Both **to** and **from** are set to one by default.

The third argument is **by**. The argument **by** gives the value by which to increment the sequence. The argument can also take on logical, numeric, and complex values; however, it cannot equal **FALSE** since **FALSE** coerces to zero and **by** cannot equal zero. The argument does not have to divide into the difference between **to** and **from** evenly. The sequence will stop at the largest value less than or equal to **to** if **to** is greater than **from**. If **to** is less than **from**, then **by** must be negative and the sequence stops at the smallest value greater than or equal to **to**.

The fourth argument is **length.out**. By default, **length.out** is set to **NULL**. The argument **length.out** can be used in place of **by**. The argument gives the length of the sequence to be output. If **length.out** is specified, **by** defaults to (**to** - **from**) / (**length.out**-1).

The fifth argument is **along.with**. The argument **along.with** is also used in place of **by**. The length of the sequence to be output is given by the length of **along.with**. The sixth argument is the argument **...** for any arguments to or from lower-level functions used by seq(). Some examples follow:

```
> seq(3)
[1] 1 2 3
```

Entering just one value without a name gives a sequence from one to the largest integer less than or equal to the value for positive values or the smallest integer greater than or equal to the value if the value is negative.

```
> seq(3, 10)
[1]  3  4  5  6  7  8  9 10
```

When two values are entered without names, the first is interpreted as the **from** value, the second is interpreted as the **to** value, and **by** is set equal to one.

```
> seq(3, 10, 2)
[1] 3 5 7 9
```

When three values are entered without names, the first is interpreted as the **from** value, the second is interpreted as the **to** value, and the third is interpreted as the **by** value.

```
> seq(3, 10, len=4)
[1]  3.000000  5.333333  7.666667 10.000000
```

Here, **length.out** is shortened to **len**.

```
> seq(3, 10, along=c(1,2,1,2))
[1]  3.000000  5.333333  7.666667 10.000000
```

Here, **along.with** is shortened to **along**.

```
> seq(c(1,2,1,2))
[1] 1 2 3 4
```

If a vector with more than one element is entered as the only argument, a sequence starting with one is created, with **by** equal to one, and of length equal to the length of the vector.

```
> seq(len=4)
[1] 1 2 3 4
```

```
> seq(7,along=c(1,2,1,2))
[1]  7  8  9 10
```

```
> seq(7,len=4)
[1]  7  8  9 10
```

Entering **length.out** or **along.with** alone or with a value for **from** returns a vector staring with the value of **from**, with **by** equal to 1, and of the correct length. For long sequences, there are lower level functions that are faster. See the help page for seq(). More information about seq() can be found by entering **?seq** at the R prompt.

The Function rep()

The function rep() repeats the first argument in a pattern determined by the other the arguments. The first argument can be any type of object that can be coerced to a vector. The other three arguments are **times**, **each**, and **length.out**. The default values for **times**, **each**, and **length.out** in the S3 system are **1**, **1**, and **NA**, respectively.

The argument **times** is a vector of values that can be coerced to integer. The argument must be either a single value or of the same length as the first argument. If the argument takes a single value, the first argument is repeated the number of times of the single value.

If the argument **times** is of length equal to the length of the first argument, then each element of the first argument is repeated the number of times indicated by the corresponding element of the argument **times**. The argument **times** is the second argument to rep(). For example:

```
> rep(0,5)
[1] 0 0 0 0 0

> rep(1:3, 5)
 [1] 1 2 3 1 2 3 1 2 3 1 2 3 1 2 3

> rep(1:3, 2:4)
[1] 1 1 2 2 2 3 3 3 3
```

Here, the second argument is not explicitly called **times**, but **times** implicitly takes on the value.

The argument **each** can be any object that can be coerced to a vector of integers, where the first element is non-negative. Only the first element of the object is used. The argument tells rep() to repeat each element of the first argument **each** times. For example:

```
> rep(1:3, each=3)
[1] 1 1 1 2 2 2 3 3 3
>
> rep(1:3, each=3, times=2)
 [1] 1 1 1 2 2 2 3 3 3 1 1 1 2 2 2 3 3 3
>
> rep( rep(1:3, times=2:4), each=2)
 [1] 1 1 1 1 2 2 2 2 2 2 3 3 3 3 3 3 3 3
>
> rep( rep(1:3, times=2:4), times=2)
 [1] 1 1 2 2 2 3 3 3 3 1 1 2 2 2 3 3 3 3
```

The last argument is **length.out**. The argument can take on any value that can be coerced to an integer vector and for which the first element is non-negative. Only the first element is used. If **length.out** is set to a value, only the number of elements given by the value of the argument is returned. For example:

```
> rep( rep(1:3, times=2:4), times=2, len=8)
[1] 1 1 2 2 2 3 3 3
```

Here, **length.out** is shortened to **len**.
More information about **rep()** can be found by entering **?rep** at the R prompt.

Combinatorics and Grid Expansion

Combinatorics is a subject about the combinations that can be made from a set of discrete values. Combinations are all of the combinations that are possible from a discrete set of values for a given number of elements in each combination, where no element is repeated. Permutations are the set of all possible permutations of a given size from a discrete set of elements. Grid expansion is about the expansion of different sets of elements so that each element of each set is linked with every element of the other sets. Probably the easiest way to see what the combinations, permutations, and grid expansion involve is by showing some examples.

Three functions that are relevant are combn(), permsn()—which is in library prob—and expand.grid. The function combn() takes the arguments **x, m, FUN, simplify**, and **...** . The argument **x** is any object that can be coerced to a vector and is the discrete set from which the combinations are formed. The argument **m** is the number of elements to include in each combination. The argument **FUN** is an optional function to operate on the elements of **x**. The argument **simplify** is logical. If **TRUE**, an array or matrix is returned. If **FALSE**, a list is returned. The default value is **TRUE**. The argument **...** contains any arguments for **FUN**. For example:

```
> combn(1:3,2)
     [,1] [,2] [,3]
[1,]    1    1    2
[2,]    2    3    3
```

Note that the combinations are down the rows.
The function permsn() is in the package **prob**. Since the package is not one of the packages installed by default, the package may need to be installed. (See Chapter 1.) If the package is installed, the package must be loaded with

```
library(prob)
```

The function permsn() takes just two arguments, **x** and **m**, which are as described for combn(). Following is an example for permsn():

```
> permsn(1:3,2)
     [,1] [,2] [,3] [,4] [,5] [,6]
[1,]    1    2    1    3    2    3
[2,]    2    1    3    1    3    2
```

Note that the permutations are down the rows. Also note that while combn() just has the combination (1,2), permsn() includes both (1,2) and (2,1) and so forth. The function permsn() returns a matrix.

The function expand.grid() takes objects as arguments. The objects are separated by commas and must be able to be coerced to a vector. The function returns the vectors crossed with each other in a data frame. For example:

```
> expand.grid(1:2,3:4,5:6)
  Var1 Var2 Var3
1    1    3    5
2    2    3    5
3    1    4    5
4    2    4    5
5    1    3    6
6    2    3    6
7    1    4    6
8    2    4    6
```

Here, the combinations are across the rows.

More information about combn(), permsn(), and expand.grid() can be found by entering **?combn**, **?prob::permsn**, and **?expand.grid** at the R prompt. Note that if **prob** is not installed, the second command will not work.

The Function Paste

This chapter ends with the function paste(). The function is used to create character strings out of any type of object. Other than the objects to be strung together, which are separated by commas, paste takes two arguments, **sep** and **collapse**. The argument **sep** gives the value of what is to separate the individual terms and is by default a white space. The argument **sep** must be a character string or character object. To set the value to nothing, set **sep** equal to *""*.

The argument **collapse** is also a character string or object and is used to separate results.

One of the useful applications of paste() is the creation of dimension names. Here is an example of three simple applications of paste(). The second example would be appropriate for creating dimension labels.

```
> paste("a", 1:3)
[1] "a 1" "a 2" "a 3"
>
> paste("a", 1:3, sep="")
[1] "a1" "a2" "a3"
>
> paste("a", 1:3, sep="", collapse="+")
[1] "a1+a2+a3"
```

You can find more information about paste() by entering **?paste** at the R prompt.

■ ■ ■

CHAPTER 10

Exporting from R

Being able to export from R makes R more useful. Objects may be exported to any connection. In this chapter we cover exporting to external files on the hard drive and to the console. You can find information about connections by entering **?connections** at the R prompt.

There are a number of functions that export to external text files, seven of which we will discuss in this chapter. The first is the function dump(). The function dump() can write named objects of any kind to an external file, but it is quite literal.

The next function is sink(). The function sink() can sink output that would normally be displayed at the console to an external file. Next is the function write(). The function write() can write atomic data to an external file. Next comes the function write.matrix(). For matrices and data frames, the function write.matrix() exports the matrix or data frame.

The next two functions are write.table() and write.csv(). For objects that can be coerced to a data frame, write.table() and write.csv() can write the object to an external file while maintaining the data frame structure. The functions are slower but more sophisticated than write.matrix().

The last function we will cover is dput(). For objects of mode function, dput() can write the contents of a function to an external file. The function deparses objects and can output other types of objects, but it is mainly used for functions.

There are also functions that convert data frames to Excel, SPSS, SAS, and Stata formats, which we brief cover in this chapter. Also, output at the console can be cut and pasted to an external file, which is often the easiest thing to do.

The Function dump()

The function dump() takes a vector of object names and exports the contents of the objects to a file. The function can be used, along with source(), to move functions from one workspace to another, but the function is more general. The function source() reads the dumped file. (For moving data rather than functions, the functions save() and load() can be used, but they save and load in binary format. See their help page for more information.)

The first argument to dump() is **list** and is a collection of the objects to be dumped. To enter the objects into the function, the object names are collected into a character vector with the object names in quotes. For example:

```
> a = function(){print(1:4)}
> b = expression(x~y)
> c = list(1:4, "a")
> d = c(1,2,3,4)

> dump(c("a","b","c","d"), file="")
a <-
function(){print(1:4)}
b <-
expression(x ~ y)
c <-
list(1:4, "a")
d <-
c(1, 2, 3, 4)
.
```

Other than the vector of named objects, the function takes the arguments **file**, **append**, **control**, **envir**, and **evaluate**.

The argument **file** contains the location to which the function writes. If the argument is set to "", the dump goes to the console. A hard drive address is an option and can be either relative to the workspace or absolute. For a hard drive address, the location is a character argument and must be contained in quotes. The default value is **"dumpdata.R"**.

The argument **append** is a logical variable. If **append** is **TRUE** and **file** equals a file name, dump() appends the dump to the existing file. If **FALSE**, the existing file is overwritten. The default value is **FALSE**.

The argument **envir** is an argument of mode function and tells dump() where to look for the objects to be dumped. The default value is **parent.frame()**.

The arguments **control** and **evaluate** have to do with saving and reloading functions by using dump() to save the function and the function source() to load the function. See the help page for dump() for a description of what **control** and **evaluate** do.

You can access the help page by entering **?dump** at the R prompt.

The Function sink()

The function sink() can send output from command line commands to a connection. The function sink() continues writing until **sink()** or **sink(file=NULL)** is entered at the R prompt. The function takes four arguments: **file**, **append**, **type**, and **split**.

The **file** argument tells sink() where to write the output. If writing to a hard drive file, the write location is a character argument, which is a hard drive address within quotes. The address can be relative to the workspace folder or absolute. The option **file=""** does not work for sink().

The second argument, **append**, tells sink() whether to append or overwrite the file. The argument is a logical argument. For **append** equal to **TRUE**, the file is appended. For **FALSE**, the file is overwritten. The default value is **FALSE**.

The third argument, **type**, tells sink() which of two possible streams to sink. The argument is a character argument, which can take on one of two values: **output** or **message**. For **output**, the output stream is sent to the file. For **message**, any messages generated by the command are sent to the file. The default value is **output**.

The fourth argument, **split**, is a logical argument that tells sink() how to split the stream. The default value is **FALSE**. See the help page for sink() for more information about **split**.

Following is an example of the use of sink():

```
> sink("test.txt")
> rnorm(10)
> sink()
```

The file "test.txt" is relative to the folder containing the R workspace. The contents of test.txt are

```
[1] -0.30618294 -0.52505474  0.47243057 -0.89954490 -1.06653790  0.03690703
[7]  1.81562861 -0.74177999 -0.28352208 -1.28133196
```

Note that the command lines are not output.

For more information, enter **?sink** at the R prompt.

The Function write()

The function write() can write atomic objects to a connection, and it writes in tabular format. The objects are entered as a one-object vector, for example, as a collection of objects collected using c(). If the data are in a matrix or array, write() reads the data down columns or dimensions of the matrix or array, but writes across rows in the two-dimensional output.

The first argument is **x**, the vector to be exported. The argument is usually any object of mode atomic.

Other than the vector to be exported, there are four more arguments to write(). The first is the character argument **file**, which tells write() where to write the output. The argument can be a location on the hard drive, relative to the workspace or absolute. If **""** is given for **file**, the output is sent to the console. The default value is **"data"**.

The second argument is **ncolumns**. The argument **ncolumns** can be logical, numeric, or complex, and if it is not an integer, it is coerced to an integer. The argument gives the number of columns for the exported table. By default, the argument takes on the value **if(is.character(x)) 1 else 5**. So if the data is of mode character, the output matrix has one column by default. Otherwise, the output matrix has five columns by default.

The input file does not have to be of a length divisible by **ncolumns**. In other words, the last row does not have to be complete.

The third argument, **append**, is a logical argument. If set to **TRUE**, the output is appended to the file. If set to **FALSE**, the file is overwritten. The default value is **FALSE**.

The fourth argument, **sep**, is a character string that gives the characters to be placed between the elements of the output matrix. The default value is a white space.

An example follows:

```
> x=1:4
> y=5:8
> z=rbind(x,y)
> w=paste("a",1:3,sep="")
> b = rep(" ",4)

> write(c(x,y,b,z,b,w), file="", ncol=4, sep=" + ")
1 + 2 + 3 + 4
5 + 6 + 7 + 8
  +   +   +
1 + 5 + 2 + 6
3 + 7 + 4 + 8
  +   +   +
a1 + a2 + a3
```

Note that when entered separately, **x** and **y** each exports as a row. When **x** and **y** are bound together into a matrix using rbind(), write() goes down the two columns to read and writes the result across the rows. Also note that there are four columns as specified by **ncol** and that there are only three elements in the last row.

You can find more information about write() by entering **?write** at the R prompt.

The Function write.matrix()

The function write.matrix() is in the package **MASS**, which is not a package that is loaded by default. **MASS** can be loaded by entering **library(MASS)** at the R prompt since **MASS** is installed by default. According to the CRAN writers, write.matrix() is much faster than write.table() for large data sets, so the function may be preferable if the matrix or data.frame is large and the data frame is appropriate.

The function has the arguments **x**, **file**, **sep**, and **blocksize**. The argument **x** is the object to be exported and should be a matrix or a data.frame containing objects of just one mode. If modes are mixed some strange things can happen. The function only exports in one mode, which is why write.matrix() is faster than write.table().

The argument **file** gives the location to which to write. For addresses on the hard drive, the argument is of mode character and is either relative to the workspace or absolute. The default value is "", which directs output to the console.

The argument **sep** is a character string that gives the separator between the outputted elements. The argument defaults to white space.

The argument **blocksize** has no default value and does not need to be entered. If entered, the argument tells write.matrix() the size of the block of data to be transferred at one time. According to the CRAN writers, the value should be as large as possible for the amount of memory available.

Here is an example. The object mat is a matrix, the object df.mat is a data frame of one mode, the object df.mat.x is a data.frame of mixed numeric and character modes.

```
> mat = matrix(1:4,2,2,dimnames=list(c("r1","r2"),c("c1","c2")))
> mat
   c1 c2
r1  1  3
r2  2  4

> write.matrix(mat)
c1 c2
1 3
2 4

> mat.df=data.frame(mat)
> mat.df
   c1 c2
r1  1  3
r2  2  4

> write.matrix(mat.df)
c1 c2
1 3
2 4

> mat.df.x = data.frame(mat,c("art","birth"))
> mat.df.x
   c1 c2 c..art....birth..
r1  1  3               art
r2  2  4             birth

> write.matrix(mat.df.x)
c1 c2 c..art....birth..
1   3           art
2   4         birth
```

More about write.matrix() can be found by entering **?MASS::write.matrix** at the R prompt.

The Functions write.table() and write.csv()

The functions write.table() and write.csv() also export matrices and data frames. The two are essentially the same function but with different defaults. All of the defaults for write.table() can be changed. For write.csv(), the defaults **append**, **col.names**, **sep**, **dec**, and **qmethod** cannot be changed. (As with read.csv() there is also the function write.csv2() for European users. The function write.csv2() uses a semicolon for the separator and a comma for the decimal point, but otherwise is the same as write.csv().)

The functions take the arguments **x, file, append**, quote, sep, eol, na, dec, **row.names, col.names**, and **qmethod**. The argument **x** is the object to be exported and must be an object that can be coerced to a data frame.

The argument **file** gives the location to which to export. For external files, **file** is of mode character and the address on the hard drive is either relative to the workspace or absolute. If **file** equals "", then the functions export to the console. The value of **file** is "" by default.

The argument **append** is a logical argument. If **append** is **TRUE**, then the file is appended with the new data frame. If **FALSE**, the file is overwritten. The default value is **FALSE**.

The argument **quote** is either logical or a numeric vector of column numbers and gives rules for placing quotes around elements. The default value is **TRUE**.

The argument **sep** is a character argument and gives the separator to be used between the elements of the exported data. The separator is entered within quotes. For read.table(), the default value is a white space. For read.csv(), the value is a comma.

The argument **eol** is an argument of mode character and gives the end of line delineator. By default, **eol** is equal to "\n". The correct value for **eol** varies with operating system. Use "\n" for Windows, "\r" for OS X, and "\r\n" for Linux.

The argument **na** is also a character argument and gives the string to be output where data is missing. The default value is **NA**.

The argument **dec** is another character argument and gives the character to be used as the decimal point. By default, **dec** equals ".".

The argument **row.names** is either a logical value or a character vector of row names. Note that write.table() and write.csv() treat the row names differently if **row. names** is set to **TRUE** or to a character vector of names. If a column of row names is in the exported data frame, the function write.table() does not create a blank character string for the name of the row name column, while write.csv() does. If **row.names** is equal to **FALSE**, there is no difference between the two with regard to row names since no row names are exported.

If no row names are given, row names are not present in the data.frame (for example, if a matrix without row names is entered for **x**) and **row.names** is **TRUE**, then the rows are given names, starting with "1" and incrementing by one with each row. By default, **row.names** equals **TRUE**.

The argument **col.names** is either logical or a character vector of column names. For write.table(), if **col.names** is set equal to **TRUE**, either the column names are taken from the data frame or, if no names are present in the data frame, column names are created starting with "V1" and incrementing the integer by one for each new column. If column names are supplied, the column names are set equal to the supplied names.

As noted above, for write.table(), by default, no value is given for the column of row names if the row name column exists in the exported file. However, if **col.names** is set equal to **NA**, then columns are treated the same as for **col.names** set equal to **TRUE** except that a blank character string is added for the row name column. If **row.names** equals **FALSE**, then setting **col.names** equal to **NA** gives an error. If **col.names** is set equal to **FALSE**, no column names are assigned in the exported file.

For write.csv(), the default for **col.names** depends on the value of **row.names**. The default cannot be changed. If **row.names** equals **TRUE**, **col.names** is set to **NA**. Otherwise, **col.names** is set equal to **TRUE**. In either case, column names are given by either the names in the data frame or, if there are no column names in the data frame, names starting with "V1" and with the integer incrementing by one for each new column.

The last argument is **qmethod** and can take on the values "escape" or "double". The default value is "escape". The argument gives instructions for double quoted values. See the help page for write.table() for more information.

Here are some examples. The object df.mat.x is a data frame with row and column names. The object mat is a matrix that does not have row or column names.

```
> df.mat.x
   c1 c2   C3
r1  1  3  art
r2  2  4 birth

> write.table(df.mat.x)
"c1" "c2" "C3"
"r1" 1 3 "art"
"r2" 2 4 "birth"

> write.table(df.mat.x, sep=",")
"c1","c2","C3"
"r1",1,3,"art"
"r2",2,4,"birth"

> write.table(df.mat.x, sep=",", col.names=NA)
"","c1","c2","C3"
"r1",1,3,"art"
"r2",2,4,"birth"

> write.table(df.mat.x, col.names=F)
"r1" 1 3 "art"
"r2" 2 4 "birth"

> write.table(df.mat.x, row.names=F, col.names=F)
1 3 "art"
2 4 "birth"

> write.table(df.mat.x, sep=",", row.names=F)
"c1","c2","C3"
1,3,"art"
2,4,"birth"

> write.csv(df.mat.x)
"","c1","c2","C3"
"r1",1,3,"art"
"r2",2,4,"birth"
```

```
> write.csv(df.mat.x, row.names=F)
"c1","c2","C3"
1,3,"art"
2,4,"birth"

> mat
     [,1] [,2]
[1,]   1    3
[2,]   2    4

> write.table(mat)
"V1" "V2"
"1" 1 3
"2" 2 4

> write.table(mat, row.names=c("r1","r2"), col.names=NA)
"" "V1" "V2"
"r1" 1 3
"r2" 2 4

> write.table(mat, row.names=F, col.names=F)
1 3
2 4

> write.csv(mat)
"","V1","V2"
"1",1,3
"2",2,4

> write.csv(mat, row.names=c("r1","r2"))
"","V1","V2"
"r1",1,3
"r2",2,4
```

To access the help page for write.table(), enter **?write.table** at the R prompt.

The Function dput()

The function dput() deparses the contents of a file and exports the result in ASCII format. Mainly dput() is used in conjunction with the function dget(), which reads the exported files. The two functions are usually used to move functions from one workspace to another.

The arguments to dput() are **x**, **file**, and **control**. The argument **x** is the file to be deparsed, usually a function.

The argument **file** tells dput() where to put the output. The value can be an address on the hard drive either absolute or relative to the workspace. If so, the argument is of character mode and the value is within quotes. By default, **file** equals "", which sends the output to the console.

The argument **control** takes character values and gives dput() more information on what to include in the export. See the help page for dput() for more information.

Here is an example using the primitive function cat(), exported to the console:

```
> dput(cat)
function (..., file = "", sep = " ", fill = FALSE, labels = NULL,
    append = FALSE)
{
    if (is.character(file))
        if (file == "")
            file <- stdout()
        else if (substring(file, 1L, 1L) == "|") {
            file <- pipe(substring(file, 2L), "w")
            on.exit(close(file))
        }
        else {
            file <- file(file, ifelse(append, "a", "w"))
            on.exit(close(file))
        }
    .Internal(cat(list(...), file, sep, fill, labels, append))
}
```

The writers at CRAN warn that the deparsing is not necessarily perfect. Also, dput() strips the attributes of the object and removes any comments. If the comments are not important, using dput() on objects of mode function should not be a problem.

You can find more information about dput()by entering **?dput** at the R prompt.

Other Exporting Functions

Like the functions that read in data, there are a variety of functions that write data. The CRAN page on importing and exporting data has much information and can be found at http://cran.r-project.org/doc/manuals/r-release/R-data.html.

For SPSS, SAS, and Stata, the function write.foreign(), which can be found in the package **foreign**, can export in the correct format. The function write.foreign() also exports in some other formats. Also, other exporting functions can be found in the package **foreign**.

The package **foreign** is one of the packages installed by default. To see the contents of **foreign**, enter **help(package=foreign)** at the R prompt. To load **foreign**, enter **library(foreign)**.

For Excel, there is a package, **xlsx**, specifically for working with Excel. The package **xlsx** is not a default package in R, so it must be installed. After **xlsx** is installed, information about **xlsx** can be found by entering **help(package=xlsx)** at the R prompt.

A search done on write() by entering **??write** at the R prompt will give some other options for exporting from R.

CHAPTER 11

■ ■ ■

Descriptive Functions and Manipulating Objects

For arrays, matrices, vectors, lists, and expressions, there are a number of functions that describe various attributes of an object. Also, there are a number of functions that manipulate objects to create new objects. The functions covered in this chapter are the descriptive functions dim(), nrow(), NROW(), ncol(), NCOL(), length(), and nchar(); and the functions that manipulate objects: cbind() and rbind(); the apply functions; sweep(), scale(), and aggregate(); the table functions; and functions tabulate(), and ftable().

Descriptive Functions

The descriptive functions describe qualities of objects. This section discusses some descriptive functions that are useful when writing functions or creating objects. The functions are dim(), nrow(), ncol(), NROW(), NCOL(), length(), and nchar().

The Function dim()

For objects for which dimensions make sense—such as matrices, data.frames, tables, or arrays—the function dim() returns the number of levels in each of the dimensions of the object. For objects of other classes, dim() returns **NULL**. An example follows:

```
> a = 1:2
> b = 1:3
>
> dim(a)
NULL

> a %o% b %o% a
, , 1

     [,1] [,2] [,3]
[1,]    1    2    3
[2,]    2    4    6

, , 2
```

```
      [,1] [,2] [,3]
[1,]    2    4    6
[2,]    4    8   12

>
> dim(a %o% b %o% a)
[1] 2 3 2
```

The dimensions of the object can be changed if the product of the original dimensions equals the product of the dimensions of the result. An example follows:

```
> a.ar = a %o% b

> a.ar
      [,1] [,2] [,3]
[1,]    1    2    3
[2,]    2    4    6

> dim(a.ar)
[1] 2 3

> dim(a.ar)= c(3,2)

> a.ar
      [,1] [,2]
[1,]    1    4
[2,]    2    3
[3,]    2    6
```

You can find more information about dim() by entering **?dim** at the R prompt.

The Functions nrow(), ncol(), NROW(), and NCOL()

For matrices, data.frames, and arrays, nrow() and ncol() give the number of levels in the first and second dimensions of the matrix, data frame, or array respectively. Other classes of objects return **NULL**. An example follows:

```
> a.ar = a%o%b

> a.ar
      [,1] [,2] [,3]
[1,]    1    2    3
[2,]    2    4    6
```

```
> nrow(a.ar)
[1] 2

> ncol(a.ar)
[1] 3

> nrow(1:20)
NULL
```

Sometimes vectors must be treated as matrices or arrays. The functions NROW() and NCOL() treat vectors as one-column matrices, but otherwise are the same as nrow() and ncol(). An example follows:

```
> NROW(1:20)
[1] 20
>
> NCOL(1:20)
[1] 1
```

You can find more information about nrow(), ncol(), NROW(), and NCOL()by entering **?nrow** at the R prompt.

The Function length()

The next descriptive function we will explain is length(). The argument to length() can be any mode of object. For atomic objects, length() returns the number of elements in the object. For list objects, length() returns the number of the top level elements. For functions, length() returns one. For calls, length() returns the number of arguments entered in the creation of the call. For names, length() returns one. For expressions, length() returns the number of elements in the expression. Some examples follow:

```
> mat=matrix(1:4,2,2)
> mat
     [,1] [,2]
[1,]    1    3
[2,]    2    4

> length(mat)
[1] 4

> a.list=list(mat, c("abc","cde"))
> a.list
[[1]]
     [,1] [,2]
[1,]    1    3
[2,]    2    4
```

```
[[2]]
[1] "abc" "cde"

> length(a.list)
[1] 2

> a.fun = function(mu, se=1, alpha=.05){
  z_value = qnorm(1-alpha/2, mu, se)
  print(z_value)
}

> length(a.fun)
[1] 1

> a.call=call("lm", y~x)
> a.call
lm(y ~ x)

> length(a.call)
[1] 2

> a.name
`1`

> length(a.name)
[1] 1

> a.exp = expression(a.call, sin(1:5/180 * pi))
> a.exp
expression(a.call, sin(1:5/180 * pi))

> length(a.exp)
[1] 2
```

The length of an atomic or list object can be assigned using length(). For other mode objects, an attempted length() assignment returns an error. If **n** is the length of an atomic object, then setting the length to a value larger than **n** generates **NA**s for the extra elements. Setting the length shorter than **n** removes the extra elements. In either case, a vector is returned unless the length is not changed, in which case the original object is returned. An example follows:

```
> mat
     [,1] [,2]
[1,]   1    3
[2,]   2    4

> mat.2 = mat
```

```
> length(mat.2)=6
> mat.2
[1]  1  2  3  4 NA NA

> mat.2 = mat

> length(mat.2)=3

> mat.2
[1] 1 2 3

> mat.2 = mat

> length(mat.2)=4

> mat.2
     [,1] [,2]
[1,]   1    3
[2,]   2    4
```

For objects of mode list, lengthening the list adds **NULL** elements at the top level while shortening the list removes elements at the top level. An example follows:

```
> a.list
[[1]]
     cl1 cl2
[1,]   1   3
[2,]   2   4

[[2]]
[1] "abc" "cde"

> length(a.list)=4

> a.list
[[1]]
     cl1 cl2
[1,]   1   3
[2,]   2   4

[[2]]
[1] "abc" "cde"

[[3]]
NULL
```

```
[[4]]
NULL

> length(a.list)=3

> a.list
[[1]]
     cl1 cl2
[1,]   1   3
[2,]   2   4

[[2]]
[1] "abc" "cde"

[[3]]
NULL
```

You can find more information about length()by entering **?length** at the R prompt.

The Function nchar()

The function nchar() counts characters in objects that can be coerced to mode character. The function takes three arguments: **x**, **type**, and **allowNA**.

The argument **x** is the object. The function coerces the object to character, and the characters to be counted are the characters of the coerced object. For example:

```
> as.character(a.list)
[1] "1:4"              "c(\"abc\", \"cde\")" "NULL"
> nchar(a.list)
[1]  3 15  4
```

Quotes are not counted.

The argument **type** is a character argument and can take on the values of **"bytes"**, **"chars"**, or **"width"**. If **"bytes"** is chosen, the bytes of the strings are counted. If **"chars"** is chosen, the standard text number of characters are counted. If **"width"** is chosen, the number of characters that the function cat() would assign the strings are counted. The default value is **"char"**. Usually there is no difference between the three.

The argument **allowNA** is a logical argument. If set equal to **TRUE**, strings that are not valid are set equal to **NA**. If set equal to **FALSE**, strings that are not valid give an error and cause the function to stop. The default value is **FALSE**.

You can find more information about nchar()by entering **?nchar** at the R prompt.

Manipulating Objects

There are a number of functions that manipulate R objects and make programming easier. This subsection covers some of the functions, including cbind(), rbind(), apply(), lapply(), sapply(), vapply(), tapply(), mapply(), sweep(), scale(), aggregate(), table(), tabulate(), and ftable().

The Functions cbind() and rbind()

The functions cbind() and rbind() are self-explanatory for vectors, matrices, data frames, and some other classes of objects such as time series. The function cbind() binds columns. The function rbind() binds rows.

For lists that are not matrixlike, the functions return the type and number of elements in each of the highest level elements of the list arguments, creating a matrix of the types with integers. Lists can be bound with non-list objects. The result will be a list, but the non-list arguments will not be converted like the list part of the result.

In the call to the function, the objects to be bound are separated by commas. For cbind(), vectors are treated as columns. For rbind(), vectors are treated as rows.

For vectors, vectors being bound do not have to be of the same length. The vectors cycle. For higher dimensional objects, the objects cycle until the bound object is filled if, for rbind(), the numbers of columns are multiples of each other and, for cbind(), the number of rows are multiples of each other. Otherwise, the functions give an error if there is a row/column mismatch.

The resulting object takes on the type of the highest level object entered, where the hierarchy, from lowest to highest, is raw, logical, integer, double, complex, character, and list.

There is one argument to cbind() and rbind() other than the objects to be bound—the argument **deparse.level**, which is used to create labels for objects that are not matrixlike. The argument is an integer argument and can take on the values of **0**, **1**, or **2**, although any value that can be coerced to an integer works. Values that do not give **1** or **2** when coerced to an integer give the same result as **0**. The default value is **1**.

For data frames, if a data frame is included in the objects to be bound and a list that is not a data frame is not included, then the result is a data frame. In that case, any character columns are changed to factors unless specified to not.

For time series, cbind() gives a multivariate time series, whereas for rbind(), the time series reverts to a matrix. An example follows:

```
> ab.list = list(one=1:5,two=3:7)
> ab.list
$one
[1] 1 2 3 4 5

$two
[1] 3 4 5 6 7
```

```
> cbind(ab.list,1:4)
    ab.list
[1,] Integer,5 1
[2,] Integer,5 2
[3,] Integer,5 3
[4,] Integer,5 4

> rbind(1:3,3:5,5:7)
    [,1] [,2] [,3]
[1,]  1    2    3
[2,]  3    4    5
[3,]  5    6    7
```

The Apply Functions

There are several functions in R for applying a function over a subset of an object, six of which are covered here. The six functions are apply(), lapply(), sapply(), vapply(), tapply(), and mapply(). The functions to be applied can be user-defined, which can be quite useful.

The Function apply()

The function apply() takes three arguments—**X**, **MARGIN**, and **FUN**—as well as any arguments to the function FUN. The first argument, **X**, is an array (including matrices). The second argument gives the margin(s) over which the function is to operate, and FUN is the function to be applied.

For matrices, entering **1** for **MARGIN** applies the function across the columns. For **2**, the function is applied down the rows.

The function to be applied is entered without parentheses. Any arguments to the function are entered next, separated by commas. The result is an array, matrix, or vector. An example follows:

```
> mat=matrix(1:4,2,2, dimnames=list(c("r1","r2"),c("c1","c2")))
> mat
   c1 c2
r1  1  3
r2  2  4

> apply(mat,1,sum)
r1 r2
 4  6

> apply(mat,1,pnorm,3,1)
          r1        r2
c1 0.02275013 0.1586553
c2 0.50000000 0.8413447
```

In the example, the arguments to pnorm( ) are the rows in mat for the **q** values, **3** for the value of **mean**, and **1** for the value of **sd**. Note that the matrix is transposed in the result.

You can find more information about apply( )by entering **?apply** at the R prompt.

The lapply(), sapply(), and vapply() Functions

The lapply( ), sapply( ), and vapply( ) functions work with vectors, including lists, and expressions. If **X** is not a list, then **X** is coerced to a list. The elements must be of the correct mode for the function being applied.

The function lapply( ) is the simplest with just two arguments plus any arguments to the function to be applied. The function sapply( ) takes four arguments plus any extra arguments for the function to be applied. The function vapply( ) also takes four arguments plus any extra for the function to be applied.

The Function lapply()

The function lapply( ) takes the arguments **X** and **FUN**, plus any extra arguments for **FUN**. The function FUN is applied to every element of the vector or every top level element of the list. The result is a list. An example follows:

```
> b.list=list(1:7,3:4)
> b.list
[[1]]
[1] 1 2 3 4 5 6 7

[[2]]
[1] 3 4

> lapply(b.list,sum)
[[1]]
[1] 28

[[2]]
[1] 7
```

You can enter arithmetic operators by enclosing the operators within quotes. For example:

```
> lapply(1:2,"^",2)
[[1]]
[1] 1

[[2]]
[1] 4
```

The Function sapply()

The function sapply() also operates on vectors, including lists, and expressions. The function takes the arguments **X** and **FUN**, then any arguments to **FUN** followed by the arguments **simplify** and **USE.NAMES**.

The argument **simplify** can be logical or the character string **"array"**. The argument **simplify** tells sapply() to simplify the list to a vector or matrix if **TRUE**, and to an array if set equal to **"array"**. No simplification is done if set equal to **FALSE**. For **FALSE**, a list is returned. The value **TRUE** is the default.

The argument **USE.NAMES** is a logical argument. For an object of mode character, the argument **USE.NAMES** tells sapply() to use the elements of the object as names for the result. The default value is **TRUE**. An example follows:

```
> ab.list
$one
[1] 1 2 3 4 5

$two
[1] 3 4 5 6 7

> sapply(ab.list, sum)
one two
 15  25

> a.char
[1] "a7"  "a8"  "a9"  "a10"

> sapply(a.char,paste,"b", sep="")
    a7     a8     a9    a10
  "a7b"  "a8b"  "a9b" "a10b"

> sapply(a.char,paste,"b", sep="", USE.NAMES=F)
[1] "a7b"  "a8b"  "a9b" "a10b"
```

The Function vapply()

The function vapply() takes the arguments **X, FUN, FUN.VALUE**, any arguments to **FUN**, and **USE.NAMES**, in that order.

The argument **FUN.VALUE** is a structure for the output from the function. The structure is the structure of the result of applying **FUN** to a single element of **X**. Dummy values of the correct mode are used in the structure. The number and mode of the dummy elements must be correct. Any extra arguments for **FUN** are placed after **FUN. VALUE**. The default value of **USE.NAMES** is **TRUE**. An example follows:

```
> set.seed(382765)
> e
[1] 1 2
```

```
> vapply(e,rnorm,matrix(.1,2,2), n=4, sd=1)
, , 1

          [,1]      [,2]
[1,] 1.701435 1.1422971
[2,] 2.068151 0.9604146

, , 2

          [,1]      [,2]
[1,] 0.3541925 1.186276
[2,] 2.6841000 1.745577
```

In the example, **e** is a vector of means entered into the function rnorm( ), and the other arguments to rnorm( ) are **n=4** and **sd=1**.

The function vapply( ) returns an array, matrix, or vector of objects of the kind given by the argument **FUN.VALUE**.

You can find more information about lapply( ), sapply( ), and vapply( ) by entering **?lapply** at the R prompt.

The Function tapply( )

The function tapply( ) applies functions to cross tabulated data. The arguments are **X**, **IND, FUN,** any extra arguments to **FUN,** and **simplify**. The default value for **FUN** is **NULL,** and the default value of **simplify** is **TRUE**.

The argument **X** must be an atomic object and is coerced to a vector. The argument can be a contingency table created by table( ). The length of **X** is then the product of the dimensions of the contingency table.

The argument **IND** must be a vector that can be coerced to a factor or a list of vectors that can be coerced to factors. The length of **X** and the length(s) of the factor vectors must all be the same.

The values of **X** are the number of observations with a given factor combination, where the factor combinations are given by crossing the factor values. If combinations are repeated, the function does not work right. There is no need to enter zeroes for factor combinations without observations, but zeroes may be included.

Using tapply( ) without a function gives the index of the cells that contain observations, while using a function gives the factor cross table, with the function applied to the contents of the cells. An example follows:

```
> list(c("a","b","b","c"), c(5,5,6,5))
[[1]]
[1] "a" "b" "b" "c"

[[2]]
[1] 5 5 6 5
```

```
> cbind(c("a","b","b","c"),c(5,5,6,5))
     [,1] [,2]
[1,] "a"  "5"
[2,] "b"  "5"
[3,] "b"  "6"
[4,] "c"  "5"

> tapply(1:4, list(c("a","b","b","c"), c(5,5,6,5)))
[1] 1 2 5 3

> tapply(1:4, list(c("a","b","b","c"), c(5,5,6,5)), "^",3)
  5  6
a 1 NA
b 8 27
c 64 NA
```

You can find more information about tapply()by entering **?tapply** at the R prompt.

The Function mapply()

The function mapply() takes an object that is a vector or a list as an argument and applies a function to each element of the vector or list. If an object that is not a vector or list is entered, mapply() attempts to coerce the object to a vector or list. The elements of the resulting object must be legal for the function to be applied. The result of mapply() is a vector, matrix, or list.

The arguments to mapply() are **FUN, . . ., MoreArgs, SIMPLIFY**, and **USE.NAMES**. The argument **FUN** is the function to be applied. The argument . . . refers to the vectors or lists on which the argument **FUN** operates and may be a collection of lists and/or vectors collected using c(). The argument **MoreArgs** refers to any additional arguments to **FUN** and by default equals **NULL**. The arguments must be in list mode, with a separate list for each argument.

The argument **SIMPLIFY** tells mapply() to attempt to simplify the result to a vector or matrix. The default value is **TRUE**. The argument **USE.NAMES** tells mapply() to use the names of the elements or, if the vector is of mode character, the characters themselves, as names for the output. By default, the value is **TRUE**. An example follows:

```
> set.seed(382765)

> a.mat = matrix(1,4,4)
> b.mat = matrix(runif(9),3,3)
> c.vec = 1:2

> mapply(det, list(a.mat, b.mat))
[1]  0.0000000 -0.3349038
```

```
> mapply(mean, c( list(a.mat,b.mat), c.vec))
[1] 1.0000000 0.6208733 1.0000000 2.0000000

> mapply(mean, c( list(a.mat,b.mat), list(c.vec)))
[1] 1.0000000 0.6208733 1.5000000
```

Here **det** finds the determinants of the elements and **mean** finds the means of the elements.

Another example—using **MoreArgs**—follows:

```
> set.seed(382765)
>
> mapply(cor, c(list(a.mat,b.mat), list(c.vec)), list(y=1:4,y=1:3,y=3:4),
list(use="everything"), list(method="pearson"))
[[1]]
      [,1]
[1,]   NA
[2,]   NA
[3,]   NA
[4,]   NA

[[2]]
           [,1]
[1,]   0.1872769
[2,]   0.8836377
[3,]  -0.4585219

[[3]]
[1] 1

Warning message:
In (function (x, y = NULL, use = "everything", method = c("pearson",  :
  the standard deviation is zero
```

Here the function is the correlation function and the arguments **y**, **use**, and **method** are supplied, each as a list.

You can find more information about mapply() by entering **?mapply** at the R prompt.

The sweep() and scale() Functions

The sweep() function operates on arrays (including matrices and vectors that have been converted to matrices), and the scale() function operates on numeric matrixlike objects. The sweep() function sweeps out a margin(s) of an array (say, the columns of a matrix) with values (say, the column means) using a function (say, the subtraction operator). The scale() function by default centers and normalizes the columns of matrices by subtracting the mean and dividing by the standard deviation for each column.

The Function sweep()

The function sweep() takes the arguments **x, MARGIN, STATS, FUN, check.margin**, and . . .. The argument **x** is the array. The array can be of any atomic mode.

The argument **MARGIN** gives the margins over which the sweep is to take place. For a matrix, **MARGIN** equals **1, 2**, or **1:2** (or **c(1,2)**). If **MARGIN** equals **1:2**, the entire matrix is swept, rather than the sweeping being done by column or row. For an array of more than two dimensions, **MARGIN** can be any subset of the margins, including all of the margins.

The argument **STATS** gives the value(s) to sweep with. For example, to use column means the function apply() can be applied; that is **apply(mat, 2, mean)** would work as a value for **STATS**, where **mat** is the matrix being swept. The value(s) for **STATS** cycle.

The argument **FUN** is the function to use. By default, **FUN** equals "-", the subtraction operator, but **FUN** can be any function legal for the values of the array. For example, **paste** can be used with arrays of mode character.

The argument **check.margin** checks to see if the dimensions or length of **STATS** agrees with the dimensions given by **MARGIN**. If not, just a warning is given. The function does not stop, but cycles the values in **STATS**. The default value is **TRUE**.

The argument . . . gives any extra arguments to the function **FUN**. An example follows:

```
> d.mat = matrix(1:8,2,4)
> d.mat
     [,1] [,2] [,3] [,4]
[1,]    1    3    5    7
[2,]    2    4    6    8

> a = sweep(d.mat, 2, apply(d.mat, 2, mean))
> a
     [,1] [,2] [,3] [,4]
[1,] -0.5 -0.5 -0.5 -0.5
[2,]  0.5  0.5  0.5  0.5

> sweep(a, 2, apply(d.mat, 2, sd), "/")
           [,1]       [,2]       [,3]       [,4]
[1,] -0.7071068 -0.7071068 -0.7071068 -0.7071068
[2,]  0.7071068  0.7071068  0.7071068  0.7071068
```

Since **MARGIN** is set equal to **2**, the function mean() takes the mean of each column and the function sd() takes the standard deviation of each column. In the second statement, the mean of each column is subtracted from the elements in the column. The subtraction function is the default, so it does not need to be entered. In the third statement, the centered elements in the columns are divided by the standard deviations for the columns.

Note that the function returns a matrix. You can find more information about sweep() by entering **?sweep** at the R prompt.

The Function scale()

The function scale() is used to scale columns of a matrix—that is, to center the column to a specified center and to scale the column to a specified standard deviation. The function scale() takes three arguments: **x**, **center**, and **scale**. The argument **x** is a matrix or matrixlike numeric object (for example a data frame or time series).

The argument **center** can be either logical or a numeric vector of length equal to the number of columns in **x**. If set to **TRUE**, the column mean is subtracted from each element in a column. If set to a vector of numbers, then each number is subtracted from the elements in the number's corresponding column. If set equal to **FALSE**, nothing is subtracted. The default value is **TRUE**.

The argument **scale** can also be logical or a vector of numbers. If **scale** is set equal to **TRUE**, each centered (if centering has been done) element is divided by the standard deviation of the elements in the column, where **NAs** are ignored and the division is by n-1. If set equal to a vector of numbers, each (centered) element of a column is divided by the corresponding number in the vector. Dividing by zero will give an **NaN** but will not stop the execution. If **scale** is set equal to **FALSE**, no division is done. The default value is **TRUE**. An example follows:

```
> d.mat = matrix(1:8,2,4)
> d.mat
     [,1] [,2] [,3] [,4]
[1,]   1    3    5    7
[2,]   2    4    6    8

> scale(d.mat)
           [,1]       [,2]       [,3]       [,4]
[1,] -0.7071068 -0.7071068 -0.7071068 -0.7071068
[2,]  0.7071068  0.7071068  0.7071068  0.7071068
attr(,"scaled:center")
[1] 1.5 3.5 5.5 7.5
attr(,"scaled:scale")
[1] 0.7071068 0.7071068 0.7071068 0.7071068

> e.mat = matrix(c(1:8,NA,2),2,5)
> e.mat
     [,1] [,2] [,3] [,4] [,5]
[1,]   1    3    5    7   NA
[2,]   2    4    6    8    2

> scale(e.mat, center=rep(3,5), scale=rep(4,5))
      [,1] [,2] [,3] [,4]  [,5]
[1,] -0.50 0.00 0.50 1.00    NA
[2,] -0.25 0.25 0.75 1.25 -0.25
attr(,"scaled:center")
[1] 3 3 3 3 3
attr(,"scaled:scale")
[1] 4 4 4 4 4
```

Note that scale() returns the scaled matrix, the values used to center the elements, and the values used to scale the elements.

For more information, enter **?scale** at the R prompt.

The Functions aggregate(), table(), tabulate(), and ftable()

Like the apply functions, the function aggregate() finds statistics for data groups. The functions table(), tabulate(), and ftable() create contingency tables out of data.

The Function aggregate()

The function aggregate() applies a function to the elements of an object based on the values of another object. The object to be operated on is either a time series, a data frame, or an object that can be coerced to a data frame. The values of the other object must be a list with elements that can be interpretable as factors and, at the second level, must be of length equal to the rows of the data frame or time series. The function treats data frames and time series differently.

Data Frames

For data frames, the arguments are **x**, **by**, **FUN**, . . ., and **simplify**. The argument **x** is a data frame. The argument **by** is an object of mode list consisting of elements that can be interpreted as factors. The elements of **by** are used to group the rows of **x**.

The argument **FUN** is the function to be applied and . . . are any extra arguments for that function. The argument **simplify** tells aggregate() whether to try to simplify the result to a vector or matrix. The default value is **TRUE**. The result of aggregate() for a data frame is a data frame. An example follows:

```
> x2=rep(1:2,3)
> x1=rep(1:2,3)
> y1=1:6
> y2=7:12

> a.df=data.frame(y1,y2,x1,x2)

> a.df
  y1 y2 x1 x2
1  1  7  1  1
2  2  8  2  2
3  3  9  1  1
4  4 10  2  2
5  5 11  1  1
6  6 12  2  2
```

```
> aggregate(a.df[,1:2], list(x1,x2), mean)
  Group.1 Group.2 y1 y2
1       1       1  1  3  9
2       2       2  2  4 10
```

For data frames, a formula may be used to classify **x** rather than using the argument **by**. For the formula option, the arguments are **formula, data, FUN, . . ., subset**, and **na. action**. The argument **formula** takes the form **y~x**, where **y** is numeric and can have more than one column and **x** is a formula such as **x1** or **x1+x2**, where both **x1** and **x2** can be interpreted as factors.

The argument **data** gives the name of the data frame and must be included. The argument **FUN** is the function to be applied and . . . contains any extra arguments for **FUN**. The argument **subset** gives the rows of the data frame on which to operate. The argument **na.action** gives the choice for how to handle missing values and is a character string. The default value is **"na.omit"**, which tell aggregate() to omit missing values. An example follows:

```
>  a.df
  y1 y2 x1 x2
1  1  7  1  1
2  2  8  2  2
3  3  9  1  1
4  4 10  2  2
5  5 11  1  1
6  6 12  2  2

> aggregate(cbind(y1,y2)~x1+x2, data=a.df, sum, subset=1:3)
  x1 x2 y1 y2
1  1  1  4 16
2  2  2  2  8
```

Note that the **by** variable must be a list while the right side of a formula cannot be a list.

Time Series

Time series have both a frequency and a period. In R, the frequency is the inverse of the period and vice versa. For example, a year can be the period of interest. Then the months have a frequency of 12 while having sub-periods of 1/12.

For time series, the arguments are **x, nfrequency, FUN, ndeltat, ts.eps**, and . . .. The argument **x** must be a time series. The argument **nfrequency** is the number of sub-periods for each period after **FUN** has operated on the time series. The value must divide evenly into the original time series frequency. The argument equals **1** by default. (The original time series frequency divided by **nfrequency** gives the number of elements that are grouped together—on which **FUN** operates.)

The argument **FUN** is the function to be applied and . . . gives any extra arguments to **FUN**. The argument . . . is at the end of the argument list. The function **FUN** must be legal for the values of the time series and is by default **sum**.

The argument **ndeltat** tells aggregate() the length of the sub-periods for the output and equals **1** by default. The product of the frequency of the original time series and **ndelta**t must be an integer.

Either **nfrequency** or **ndeltat** can be set. The other is set to the inverse of the one set.

The argument **ts.eps** gives the tolerance for accepting that **nfrequency** divides evenly into the frequency of the time series. By default, **nfrequency** equals getOption("ts.eps"), which value can be found by entering **options("ts.eps")** at the R prompt. The value is numeric and can be set manually. An example follows:

```
> x1=c(1,2,1,2,1,2)
> x2=c(1,2,3,1,2,3)

> a.ts=ts(cbind(x1,x2), start=1, frequency=3)
> a.ts
Time Series:
Start = c(1, 1)
End = c(2, 3)
Frequency = 3
          x1 x2
1.000000   1  1
1.333333   2  2
1.666667   1  3
2.000000   2  1
2.333333   1  2
2.666667   2  3

> aggregate(a.ts, FUN=sum)
Time Series:
Start = 1
End = 2
Frequency = 1
  x1 x2
1  4  6
2  5  6
```

Note that in the example, **nfrequency** and **ndeltat** both equal one.

You can find more information about aggregate() by entering **?aggregate** at the R prompt.

The Functions table(), as.table(), and is.table()

There are three functions associated with creating tables using table(). The function table() creates a contingency table from atomic data or some lists. The data must be able to be interpreted as factors. The result has class table. The function as.table() attempts to coerce an object to class table. The function is.table() tests if an object is of class table.

The arguments to table() are **...**, **exclude**, **useNA**, **dnn**, and **deparse.level**.

The argument . . . refers to the object(s) that are to be cross-classified. The objects are separated by commas and, for atomic objects, must have same length. For list objects, the second level elements must all have the same length and be atomic. Atomic and list objects cannot be combined in a call to table().

The argument **exclude** gives values to be excluded from the contingency table. By default, **exclude** equals **if(useNA=="no") c(NA, NaA)**, which tells table() not to set a level for missing values or illegal values, such as one divided by zero, if the argument **useNA** equals **"no"**.

The argument useNA is a character argument and can take on the value **"no"**, **"ifany"**, or **"always"**. For **"no"**, no level is set for missing values. For **"ifany"**, a level is set if missing values are present. For **"always"**, a level for missing values is always set. The default level is **"no"**.

The argument **dnn** is a list argument and gives dimension names for the contingency table. The default value is list.names(. . .). The function list.names() is defined in table() and gives the names of the dimensions being tabulated.

The argument **deparse.level** is an integer argument that can take on the values of **0, 1, or 2**. The argument controls list.names() if **dnn** is not given. For **0**, no names are given. For **1**, the column names are used. For **2**, column names are deparsed. The default value is **1**. An example follows:

```
> table(c(1,2,1,2),1:4, useNA="always", deparse.level=0)

     1 2 3 4 <NA>
1    1 0 1 0    0
2    0 1 0 1    0
<NA> 0 0 0 0    0

> table(c(1,2,1,NA),1:4,c(5,6,6,5), useNA="no", deparse.level=1)
, ,  = 5

  1 2 3 4
1 1 0 0 0
2 0 0 0 0

, ,  = 6

  1 2 3 4
1 0 0 1 0
2 0 1 0 0

> table(c(1,2,1,NA),1:4,c(5,6,6,5), useNA="ifany", deparse.level=2)
, , c(5, 6, 6, 5) = 5
```

```
            1:4
c(1, 2, 1, NA) 1 2 3 4
           1   1 0 0 0
           2   0 0 0 0
         <NA> 0 0 0 1

, , c(5, 6, 6, 5) = 6

            1:4
c(1, 2, 1, NA) 1 2 3 4
           1   0 0 1 0
           2   0 1 0 0
         <NA> 0 0 0 0
```

Note that the first and last arrays have four non-zero elements, but the second array only has three since the NA is excluded.

The function as.table() takes the arguments **x** and .... The argument **x** is the object to be coerced to class table. The argument must be of mode numeric. The argument... provides any arguments for lower-level functions.

The function is.table() takes the argument **x** and returns **TRUE** if **x** is of class table and **FALSE** if not.

You can find more information about table(), as.table(), and is.table() by entering **?table()** at the R prompt.

The Function tabulate()

The function tabulate() coerces numeric or factor objects to vectors and tabulates the result. The arguments are **bin** and **nbins**. The argument **bin** is the object to be binned. If the object is not an integer or factor object, then the elements are rounded down to integers. The resulting integers must be positive. If an illegal element is present, the element is ignored.

The argument **nbins** gives the largest integer to be binned and by default equals **max(1, bin, na.rm=T)**—that is, the largest value in **bin**, assuming the largest value in **bin** is larger than one.

If **nbins** is smaller than the largest value in **bin**, then only those values with a value less than or equal **nbins** are binned. All of the integers between one and **nbins** are binned even if there are zero elements in a given bin. The function creates a vector without labels. The bins always start with one. An example follows:

```
> tabulate(c(-3.5,.9,1,4,5.6,5.4,4,1,3))
[1] 2 0 1 2 2

> tabulate(c(-3.5,.9,1,4,5.6,5.4,4,1,3), nbins=3)
[1] 2 0 1
```

In the example, there are two ones, zero twos, one three, two fours, and two fives in the reduced object.

The function tabulate() is good when all of the bins, including those with zero elements, are needed. You can find more information about tabulate() by entering **?tabulate** at the R prompt.

The Function ftable()

The function ftable() creates a matrix out of a contingency table—that is, a matrix that is a flat table. The arguments are . . ., **exclude**, **row.vars**, and **col.vars**. The argument . . . can be objects that can be coerced to a vector and that can be interpreted as factors. The argument can be a list whose elements can be interpreted as factors, or the argument can be of class table or ftable.

The argument **exclude** gives the values to be excluded when building the flat table. By default, **exclude** equals **c(NA, NaN)**.

The arguments **row.vars** and **col.vars** give the dimensions to put in the rows and columns. The values can go from one to the number of dimensions in the table—in other words, a table with three dimensions can have **row.vars** and **col.vars** equal to **1:2** and **3**; or **2:1** and **3**; or **1** and **3**; or **c(3,1)** and **2**; and so forth. An example follows:

```
> a.list = list(1:2,3:4,5:6)
> ftable(a.list)
        x.3 5 6
x.1 x.2
1   3       1 0
    4       0 0
2   3       0 0
    4       0 1

> a1 = 1:2
> a2 = 3:4
> a3 = 5:6
> ftable(a1, a2, a3, row.vars=3, col.vars=2:1)
   a2 3   4
   a1 1 2 1 2
a3
5     1 0 0 0
6     0 0 0 1

> a.table = table(1:2,3:4,5:6)
> ftable(a.table, row.vars=2, col.vars=3)
   5 6

3  1 0
4  0 1
```

You can find more information about ftable() by entering **?ftable** at the R prompt.

■ ■ ■

Flow Control

Part V covers the flow control commands and functions. Flow control involves directing the flow of a function based on conditions. In R, the flow control statements are **for, while, if, if/else**, and **repeat**. The flow control functions are ifelse() and switch().

Many computer languages use similar flow control, but in R it is usually easier and faster to use indices rather than flow control. Chapter 13 gives examples of the two approaches.

Chapter 12 describes the five flow control commands and the way to use the commands. It also describes the use of the statements **break** and **next**.

Chapter 13 gives five examples using the control commands, each of which is accompanied by a counterexample of the same exercise using indices.

Chapter 14 gives descriptions and examples of the flow control functions ifelse() and switch().

■ ■ ■

CHAPTER 12

Flow Control

Flow control statements are used to repeat a series of tasks a number of times or to direct flow based on a logical object. For persons who came into programming in the age of FORTRAN and BASIC, using loops is very comfortable. In R, the better choice, if possible, is to use arrays and index selection instead of looping. Using indices is much faster than looping.

That said, the control statements are **if**, **if/else**, **while**, **for**, and **repeat**. They are sometimes necessary and often useful. In this chapter, we give syntax for the flow control statements. We give examples of the use of flow control in Chapter 13.

Brackets "{}" and the Semicolon ";"

Curly brackets are used to enclose sections of code. Brackets can be used with **if**, **while**, **for**, and **repeat** flow control statements to delineate the section of code on which the control statement is to operate, both within functions and at the R console.

Brackets can also be used without an accompanying flow control statement, directly at the R console. Starting with an opening bracket, code statements can be entered one line at a time. The statements do not execute until the closing bracket is entered.

The semicolon is used to include more than one statement on one line. A statement is not evaluated until the statement before it has finished executing. If the first statement is a flow control statement followed by a single statement of code, the control flow must finish before the second statement executes. However, if the two—or more—statements are enclosed in an opening and a closing bracket after a flow control statement, all of the statements within the brackets are executed together based on the flow control statement.

The "if" and "if/else" Control Statements

The **if** control statement takes a logical object and executes code if the object is true. If the object is not true, then, optionally, different code given by an **else** executes.

The logical object must be an object that can be coerced to logical. If the logical object is of length greater than one, only the first element of the object is used.

The **if** statement can take the following forms:

```
if ('logical object') 'single code statement'

if ('logical object') 'single code statement';'single code statement'

if ('logical object') {'more than one code statement separated by semicolons'}

if ('logical object') {
'lines of code statements'
}
```

These four forms are not exhaustive of the possible forms. In the second form, the second statement will execute even if the logical object is false since the two statements are not enclosed in brackets.

If the **logical object** is false, then the option exists to have R execute different code by using an **else** statement. For the two control statements **if** and **else**, two examples of form follow:

```
if ('logical object') 'single code statement' else 'single code statement'

if ('logical object') {
'lines of the code statements'
}
else {
'lines of the code statements'
}
```

Again, the two forms are not exhaustive. If no **else** control statement is present and **logical object** is false, then the code statements following the **if** statement are skipped.

The "while" Control Statement

The **while** control statement executes a block of code while a logical condition is true. Again, the logical object must be an object that can be coerced to logical. If the logical object is of length greater than one, only the first element of the object is used.

The control statement can take the following forms:

```
while ('logical object') 'single code statement'

while ('logical object') 'single code statement'; 'single code statement'

while ('logical object') {'multiple code statements separated by semicolons'}

while ('logical object') {
'lines of code statements'
}
```

Again, the forms shown are not exhaustive of the possible forms. Note that for the second form, the second statement does not execute until the while loop is ended since the two statements are not in brackets.

The "for" Control Statement

The **for** control statement instructs R to loop through a section of code for a set number of times. There are a number of ways that the looping can be done based on the looping criteria.

The looping criteria can be quite flexible. The simplest form is

```
for (i in 1:n)
```

where **i** is an object that indexes from **1** to **n** and where **n** is an integer.

In general, the syntax of the flow control statement for **for** loops is

```
for ('indexing variable' in 'vector object')
```

where **indexing variable** is a variable whose value changes at each iteration of the loop and **vector object** contains the values that **indexing value** takes. The vector object can be any object that can be coerced to a vector, including objects of mode list and expression.

The object indexing variable will take on the values of **vector object** sequentially. Usually, the indexing variable is used in the code statements executed by the **for** loop.

Note that if the vector object is created using the function seq() within the **for** statement and the seq() argument **along.with**—which can be abbreviated **along**—is used, seq() gives the indices of the elements of **along.with** rather than the values of the object.

Some forms of a **for** loop are the following:

```
for ('looping criteria') 'single code statement'

for ('looping criteria') 'single code statement'; 'single code statement'

for ('looping criteria') {'multiple code statements separated by semicolons'}

for ('looping criteria') {
'lines of code statements'
}
```

Again, the four forms are not exhaustive of the possible forms. In the second form, the code after the semicolon does not execute until after the **for** loop is finished since the two statements are not in brackets.

According to the CRAN help page for flow control, the value of the indexing variable can be changed in the code statements referenced by **for** but, at the start of the next loop, reverts to the next indexed value of the variable. At the end of the looping, the value of **indexing variable** is the final value of the indexing variable in the loop.

The "repeat" Control Statement

The **repeat** flow control statement repeats a section of code until a stopping point is reached. The stopping point must be programmed into the section of code. Unlike **while**, **repeat** does not have a logical object as part of the control statement and, unlike **for**, no looping index is part of the control statement. Following are two forms for repeat:

```
repeat {'some code statements separated by semicolons'}

repeat {
'lines of code statements'
}
```

Again, the two are not exhaustive. Infinite loops are possible with **repeat**, so use caution.

The Statements "break" and "next"

The statements **break** and **next** are used for flow control within those sections of code controlled by one of the flow controllers.

The statement **break** tells R to leave a **for**, **while**, or **repeat** loop or an **if** section and go to the first statement after the loop or section.

The statement **next** tells R to stop executing the code statements in a **for**, **while**, or **repeat** loop and start again at the beginning of the loop—with the value of the indexing variable, if there is one, taking on the next value of the variable.

Nesting

Any of the flow control statements can be nested within other flow control sections of code. For the sake of clarity and to prevent subtle bugs, use brackets at all levels when nesting flow control sections within other flow control sections.

Most of the information presented here on flow control is from the CRAN help page on controlling flow, which can be found by entering **?"if"** at the R prompt.

■ ■ ■

CHAPTER 13

Examples of Flow Control

This chapter gives some examples of flow control as well as ways to do the examples using indexing. The first example uses nested **for** loops and **if/else** statements. The second example uses the **while** statement. The third example is of nested **for** loops. The fourth example uses a **for** loop, an **if** statement, and a **next** statement. The fifth example is of a **for** loop, a **repeat** loop, an **if** statement, and a **break** statement.

Nested 'for' Loops with an 'if/else' Statement

In this example, we do an element-by-element substitution into a matrix based on an **if/else** test.

First, a two-by-five matrix **x** is generated and the matrix is displayed. Next, two **for** loops cycle through the row and column indices of **x**. At each cycle, a set of **if/else** statements test whether the element in the matrix is greater than five.

If the value of the element is greater than five, the value of the element is replaced with one. If not, control goes to the **else** statement. Within the **else** statement, the value of the element is replaced by zero.

Last, the resultant matrix is displayed. The example follows:

```
> x = matrix(1:10,2,5)

> x
     [,1] [,2] [,3] [,4] [,5]
[1,]    1    3    5    7    9
[2,]    2    4    6    8   10

> for (i in 1:2) {
+    for (j in 1:5) {
+       if ( x[i,j]>5 ) x[i,j]=1
+       else x[i,j]=0
+    }
+ }

> x
     [,1] [,2] [,3] [,4] [,5]
[1,]    0    0    0    1    1
[2,]    0    0    1    1    1
```

Using Indices

Doing the same substitution without loops is easier. First, the matrix **x** is generated and displayed. Next, a second matrix, **y**, is set equal to **x**. The matrix **y** is used to hold the values of **x** since the values of **x** are changed in two steps. Next, the elements in **x** are set equal to the new values based on the original values—which are in **y**. Last, the resultant matrix is displayed. The example follows:

```
> x = matrix(1:10,2,5)

> x
     [,1] [,2] [,3] [,4] [,5]
[1,]    1    3    5    7    9
[2,]    2    4    6    8   10

> y=x

> x[y>5] = 1
> x[y<=5] = 0

> x
     [,1] [,2] [,3] [,4] [,5]
[1,]    0    0    0    1    1
[2,]    0    0    1    1    1
```

On my computer, using a matrix with 43,830 rows and 35 columns, the looping method took around five seconds and the indexing method took under a second.

A 'while' Loop

In this example, a **while** loop is used to find how many iterations it takes for a sum of variables distributed randomly and uniformly between zero and one to be greater than five.

After initially setting the seed for the random number generator and setting **n** and **x** to zero, a **while** loop is started to increment **n** and to sum **x**. A number generated using the random number generator for the uniform distribution is added to **x** at each iteration. When **x** is greater than five, the looping stops. The values for **n** and **x** are printed out. The example follows:

```
> set.seed(129435)

> n=0
> x=0
```

```
> while (x<=5) {
+    x = x + runif(1)
+    n = n + 1
+ }

> n
[1] 7

> x
[1] 5.179325
```

Using Indices

To do the same task using indices, a vector of uniform random variables is generated of length greater than what would be expected for the result of the sum.

Then the function cumsum(), which creates a cumulative sum along a vector, is used to find when the sum is greater than five. Since the elements of **x** are always greater than zero, the accumulated sum always increases along the vector.

Next, the function length() is used to find the number of elements for which the sum is less than or equal to five. Then the values for **n** and **x** are printed out, where **x** equals **x[n]**.

```
> set.seed(129435)

> x = runif(25)
> x = cumsum(x)
> n = length(x[x<=5])+1
> x = x[n]

> n
[1] 7

> x
[1] 5.179325
```

Note that the random number generator is set to the same seed value for both parts of the example, so the results for the two match since the same first seven numbers are generated.

On my computer, if I substitute 1,000,000 for 5 in the examples above, and 3,000,000 for 25, the method using indices is almost instantaneous, while the method using looping takes about nine seconds.

Nested 'for' Loops

Sometimes the differences between each of the columns of a matrix are needed. In this example, nested **for** loops are used to find the differences.

First, a matrix **x** is generated with two rows and four columns and is assigned column names. Next, the matrix is displayed. Then a matrix **xp** of zeroes with two rows and six columns is generated to hold the result of the differences, and the matrix is assigned blank column names.

Next, a counter **k** for the columns in the matrix **xp** is set to zero. As the two **for** loops increment, **k** will increase by one at each step.

Then the two **for** loops are run. In the loops, the elements of **xp** are filled with differences between different the columns in **x**. The two loops loop through the columns in the matrix **x** in such a way that no column combinations are repeated and the two columns are never the same. At each step, the columns of **xp** are assigned names based on the names in **x**.

Last, the resulting matrix **xp** is displayed. The example follows:

```
> x = matrix(1:8,2,4)
> colnames(x) = paste("c", 1:4, sep="")
> x
     c1 c2 c3 c4
[1,]  1  3  5  7
[2,]  2  4  6  8

> xp = matrix(0,2,6)
> colnames(xp) = rep("",6)
> xp

[1,] 0 0 0 0 0 0
[2,] 0 0 0 0 0 0

> k=0

> for (i in 1:3) {
+   for (j in (i+1):4) {
+     k = k+1
+     xp[,k] = x[,i]-x[,j]
+     colnames(xp)[k] = paste(colnames(x)[i], "-", colnames(x)[j], sep="")
+   }
+ }
>
> xp
     c1-c2 c1-c3 c1-c4 c2-c3 c2-c4 c3-c4
[1,]    -2    -4    -6    -2    -4    -2
[2,]    -2    -4    -6    -2    -4    -2
```

Note that the number of columns in **xp** equals p(p-1)/2, where **p** is the number of columns in **x**.

Using Indices

To do this problem using indices, two vectors of indices are created.

First, the initial matrix **x** is generated, assigned column names, and displayed. Then two sets of indices of the same length, **ind.1** and **ind.2**, are created. The respective indices in the two sets are never the same and all possible combinations are present and present only once.

Next, the resultant matrix **xp** is created by subtracting the columns of **x** in the second index set from the columns of **x** in the first index set. Next, the column names for **xp** are created and assigned using paste() and the two index sets.

Last, the matrix **xp** is displayed. The example follows:

```
> x = matrix(1:8,2,4)
> colnames(x) = paste("c", 1:4, sep="")
> x
     c1 c2 c3 c4
[1,]  1  3  5  7
[2,]  2  4  6  8

> ind.1 = rep(1:3,3:1)
> ind.1
[1] 1 1 1 2 2 3

> ind.2 = 2:4
> for(i in 3:4) ind.2 = c(ind.2,i:4)
> ind.2
[1] 2 3 4 3 4 4

> xp = x[,ind.1] - x[,ind.2]
> colnames(xp) = paste("c", ind.1, "-","c", ind.2, sep="")

> xp
     c1-c2 c1-c3 c1-c4 c2-c3 c2-c4 c3-c4
[1,]   -2    -4    -6    -2    -4    -2
[2,]   -2    -4    -6    -2    -4    -2
```

Note that a **for** loop is used to create the second set of indices. Also, column indices are repeated in both sets of indices.

For large matrices, the second method is faster than the first. On my computer, column differences for two matrices each with 43,830 rows and 35 columns were found by the two methods. The two methods both gave the same 43,830-by-595 matrix. The looping method took around 1.5 seconds and the indexing method took around 1.0 second.

A 'for' Loop, 'if' Statement, and 'next' Statement

In this example, standard normal random numbers are generated and compared to 1.965. Only those values that are less than or equal to 1.965 are kept.

First, the seed for the random number generator is set to an arbitrary value. Then a single standard normal number is generated. (We ignore the possibility that the number is greater than 1.965.) In the **for** loop that comes next, for 10,000 iterations a standard normal random number is generated at each iteration. If the number is larger than 1.965, the next loops starts. Otherwise, the number is added to a vector of numbers. A histogram is plotted of the final vector. See Figure 13-1 for the result. The example follows:

```
> set.seed(69785)
>
> x = rnorm(1)
>
> for (i in 1:10000) {
+    x2 = rnorm(1)
+    if (x2>1.965) next
+    x = c(x, x2)
+ }
>
> hist(x)
```

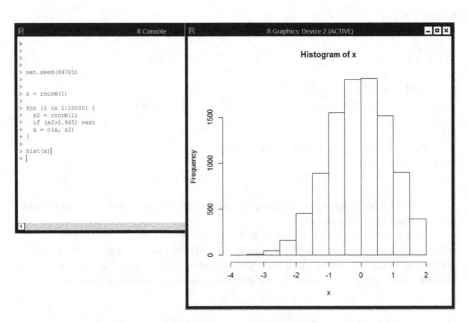

Figure 13-1. *Using a loop to generate a histogram of random standard normal variates that are less then 1.965*

Using Indices

Using indices is much simpler. First, the random number generator seed is set to the same value as for the previous example. Next, a vector of standard normal random variables of length 10,001 is generated. Next, only those values in the vector that are less than or equal to 1.965 are kept. Last, a histogram of the vector is generated. The histogram is shown in Figure 13-2. The example follows:

```
> set.seed(69785)
>
> x = rnorm(10001)
> x = x[ x<=1.965 ]
>
> hist(x)
```

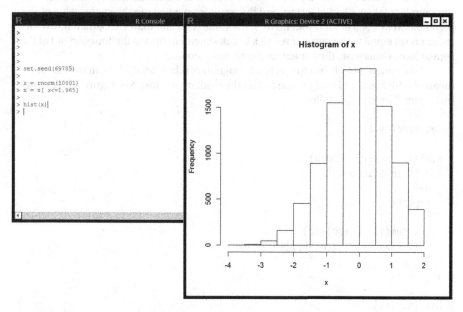

Figure 13-2. *Using indices to generate a histogram of random standard normal variates that are less then 1.965*

Note that the two histograms are the same since the seeds are the same and the same 10,001 numbers are used.

If 10,000 is increased to 100,000 above, on my computer the method using loops takes about 13 seconds while the method using indices takes less than 1 second.

A 'for' Loop, a 'repeat' Loop, an 'if' Statement, and a 'break' Statement

In this example, random samples of size 100 of standard normal numbers are generated within a **repeat loop**, which is within a **for** loop that goes through 10,000 iterations.

For each sample, the sum of the sample is divided by the square root of 100 and then compared to 1.965. If the value is less than 1.965, then the **repeat** loop continues. Otherwise, the **repeat** loop stops, the number of times through the loop is recorded, and the next **for** loop starts. At the end, the vector of the numbers of times through the loop is plotted in a histogram and the mean and median of the numbers of times is found.

First, the seed for the random number generator is set. Then a vector **n.hist** is created to hold the results, with a space for each iteration of the **for** loop. Next, the **for** loop opens and the counter **n** is set to zero. Then the **repeat** loop opens.

At the beginning of the **repeat** loop, the counter **n** is incremented by one. Then the sample is taken, divided by ten, and the result is set equal to **x**. Next, the value of **x** is compared to 1.965 in an **if** statement. If the value is greater than 1.965, then **n.hist** for index **i** is set equal to the counter **n** and a **break** statement breaks the function out of the **repeat** loop. Otherwise, the **repeat** loop continues looping.

At the end, hist() is run to create a histogram of **n.hist**, mean() is run to find the mean of **n.hist**, and median() is run to find the median of **n.hist**. See Figure 13-3 for the histogram. The example follows:

```
> set.seed(69785)

> n.hist = numeric(10000)
> for (i in 1:10000) {
+    n=0
+    repeat{
+       n=n+1
+       x=sum(rnorm(100)/10)
+       if (x>1.965) {n.hist[i]=n; break}
+    }
+ }

> hist(n.hist)

> mean(n.hist)
[1] 40.4769

> median(n.hist)
[1] 28
```

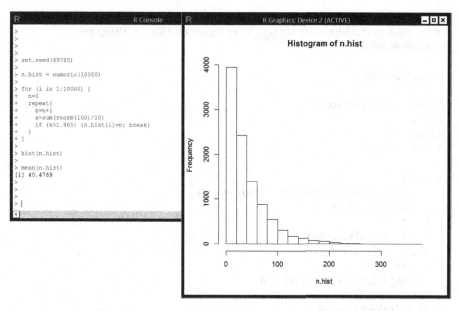

Figure 13-3. *The numbers of times needed until the result exceed 1.965 for sums of 100 standard normal variable divided by 10—using a for loop*

Note that the mean is close to 40, which is the expected number of trials necessary on average to see an event with a probability of 0.025 of occurring. However, the median is much smaller since the distribution is highly skewed.

Using Indices

To do this example using indices, we found the **repeat** loop necessary, but that the **for** loop could be dispensed with.

Once again, the random number generator seed is set—to the same number as in the first part of the example—and **n.hist** is defined **numeric** with 10,000 elements. Then the counter **n** is set to zero, the counter **cl.sv** is set to zero, and the counter **n.col** is set to 10,000.

Next, the **repeat** loop opens. The matrix **x** is defined as a matrix with 100 rows and **n.col** columns (initially 10,000). The elements of **x** are 100 times **n.col** randomly generated standard normal numbers.

Next, the function apply() is used to sum each column of the matrix, and the result is assigned to **x**. Then each element of **x** is divided by 10. Next, the length of the vector containing those elements of **x** that are larger than 1.965 is assigned to **x**.

Then **x** is added to **cl.sv** and **n** is incremented by one. Next, values of **n.hist** are set equal to **n**, where **cl.sv** and **x** are used to say where along the vector **n.hist** to put the value of **n**.

Next, **n.col** is decremented by the value of **x**. The **repeat** loop continues until **n.col** equals zero.

The histogram of **n.hist** is generated using hist(), the mean of **n.hist** using mean(), and the median of **n.hist** using median(). See Figure 13-4 for the histogram. The example follows:

```
> set.seed(69785)

> n.hist = numeric(10000)
> n = 0
> cl.sv = 0
> n.col = 10000

> repeat{
+    x = matrix(rnorm(n.col*100), 100, n.col)
+    x = apply(x, 2, sum)
+    x = x/10
+    x = length(x[x>1.965])
+    cl.sv = cl.sv + x
+    n = n+1
+    n.hist[(cl.sv-x+1):cl.sv] = n
+    n.col = n.col-x
+    if (n.col==0) break
+ }

> hist(n.hist)

> mean(n.hist)
[1] 40.5015

> median(n.hist)
[1] 28
```

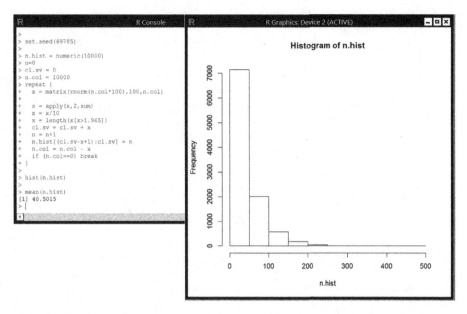

Figure 13-4. *The numbers of times needed to exceed 1.965 for sums of 100 standard normal variable divided by 10—using indices*

Once again, the mean is close to 40 and the median is 28.

Both methods use about the same amount of time. If 10,000 is replaced by 100,000 above, then the looping method takes about 53 seconds and the indexing method takes about 56 seconds on my computer.

Since the process of generating the random samples is different between the two methods—the second method generates more numbers than the first—the results for the two methods are not identical even though the seed for the random number generator is the same.

■ ■ ■

CHAPTER 14

The Functions ifelse( ) and switch( )

The two functions ifelse( ) and switch( ) execute flow control within a function. The function ifelse( ) evaluates a logical expression and chooses one of two values based on the result. The function switch( ) takes a value as an argument and returns another value based on the value of the first argument.

The Function ifelse( )

The ifelse( ) function takes three arguments. The first is a logical object or any object that can be coerced to logical, such as objects of the atomic modes or objects of mode list where there is only one level of depth to the list and where each element takes on only one value. Also, you can use a function that returns values that can be coerced to logical. The second argument is the value(s) to be returned where the first argument is true. The third argument is the value(s) to be returned where the first argument is false.

Each element of the first argument is tested separately. Elements of mode character and missing elements return **NA**. Otherwise, the value that is returned for a given element is the value in the same position in the second (or third) argument. For example, if the first argument is the vector (T,T,F,T), the second argument is the vector (1,2,1,2), and the third argument is (4,5,6,4), then ifelse( ) returns (1,2,6,2). That is:

```
> ifelse(c(T,T,F,T), c(1:2,1:2), c(4:6,4))
[1] 1 2 6 2
```

If possible, the result has the same dimensions as the first argument. Otherwise, a vector of mode list of length equal to the length of the first argument is returned. For example:

```
> a.mat = matrix(0:3,2,2)
> a.mat
     [,1] [,2]
[1,]    0    2
[2,]    1    3
```

```
> a.list = list(a.mat,c("a","b","c"))
> a.list
[[1]]
     [,1] [,2]
[1,]   0    2
[2,]   1    3

[[2]]
[1] "a" "b" "c"

> ifelse(a.mat,1:4,30:33)
     [,1] [,2]
[1,]  30    3
[2,]   2    4

> ifelse(a.mat,1:4,a.list)
[[1]]
     [,1] [,2]
[1,]   0    2
[2,]   1    3

[[2]]
[1] 2

[[3]]
[1] 3

[[4]]
[1] 4
```

Note that in the second call to ifelse(), the first element of **a.mat** results in a **FALSE** and the first element of **a.list** is a matrix, so a list is generated.

If the first argument is of length less than the length of the second (or third) argument, only those elements in the second (or third) argument up to the length of the first argument will be used. For example:

```
> ifelse(c(T,F), 1:5, 10:15)
[1] 1 11
```

The first element of **1:5** is **1** and the second element of **10:15** is **11**, so (1,11) is returned.

If the first argument is of length longer than the second (or third) argument, the second (or third) argument cycles. For example:

```
> ifelse(c(T,F,F,F,T), 1:3, 10:12)
[1] 1 11 12 10 2
```

The second argument cycles to $(1,2,3,1,2)$ and the third argument cycles to $(10,11,12,10,11)$.

If the modes of the resulting elements are not the same, then the result will have the mode of the element with the highest hierarchy, where the hierarchy goes—from lowest to highest—logical, integer, double, complex, character, and list. Objects of mode **NULL** and raw give an error. For example:

```
> ifelse(c(T,F,F,F,T), 1:5+1i, 1:5)
[1] 1+1i 2+0i 3+0i 4+0i 5+1i

> ifelse(c(T,F,F,F,T), as.raw(2:6), as.raw(12:16))
Error in ifelse(c(T, F, F, F, T), as.raw(2:6), as.raw(12:16)) :
  incompatible types (from raw to logical) in subassignment type fix
```

A function can be used as the value for any of the three arguments. If the function is evaluated, the result of the function is returned first. The last result is the result of the substitution. For example:

```
> f.fun = function(mu, se=1, alpha=.05){
  q_value = qnorm(1-alpha/2, mu, se)
  print(q_value)
}

> ifelse (f.fun(1:2, alpha=1.0), f.fun(1:2), f.fun(3))
[1] 1 2
[1] 2.959964 3.959964
[1] 2.959964 3.959964

> ifelse (f.fun(0:2, alpha=1.0), f.fun(1:2), f.fun(3))
[1] 0 1 2
[1] 2.959964 3.959964
[1] 4.959964
[1] 4.959964 3.959964 2.959964
```

Note that in the first call to f.fun(), alpha is set to 1.0, so the median is returned. Also, in the first call, the first two functions are evaluated while in the second call all three functions are evaluated.

If the result is assigned to an object, then the results of the functions are printed at the console, but the result of the ifelse() is passed to the object. For example:

```
> a=ifelse (f.fun(1:2, alpha=1.0), f.fun(1:2), f.fun(3))
[1] 1 2
[1] 2.959964 3.959964
> a
[1] 2.959964 3.959964
```

The function ifelse() can be nested. For example, a first order Markov chain of length six with two states, where the transition matrix is

$$\begin{bmatrix} 0.7 & 0.3 \\ 0.8 & 0.2 \end{bmatrix}$$

can be generated using nested ifelse() functions. That is, letting "A" be the first state and "B" be the second state:

```
> set.seed(6978)
> mc="A"

> for (i in 2:6) {
+    rn = runif(1)
+    mc = c(mc, ifelse(mc[i-1]=="A", ifelse(rn<=0.7,"A","B"),
ifelse(rn<=0.8,"B","A")))
+ }

> mc
[1] "A" "A" "B" "B" "B" "B"
```

You can find more information about ifelse() by entering ?ifelse at the R prompt.

The Function switch()

The function switch() takes any number of arguments. The first argument tells switch() which of the following arguments to return. The arguments that follow the first argument are the objects to be returned. The first argument must be numeric, logical, complex, character or **NA**, and it must consist of a single element. The rest of the arguments can be of any mode and dimension. Commas separate the arguments.

If the first argument is numeric, the number is rounded down to an integer; if logical, **TRUE** is coerced to **1** and **FALSE** to **0**; and if complex, the imaginary part is discarded and the real part is treated like numeric.

The function returns the argument indicated by the first argument. For example, if the first argument is **3**, then the fourth argument is returned. That is:

```
> switch(3,5,"a","b",6)
[1] "b"
```

If the first argument is larger than the number of arguments minus one, is less than one, or is **NA**, then a NULL object is returned. For example:

```
> switch(0,1,2,3)
> mode(switch(0,1,2,3))
[1] "NULL"
```

A character string for the first element causes switch() to behave differently. The function looks at the names of the arguments following the character string to try to find a match. All of the following arguments must be named with the exception of one possible element without a name. (Arguments can be named in the listing by entering the name, followed by an equal sign, followed by an - optional - value.)

If there is an argument without a name, then that argument becomes the default value if there is no match to the character string. If there is no argument without a name, then the default value is a NULL object. For example:

```
> switch("e", a=1, b=2, c=3, d=4, e=f.fun(0))
[1] 1.959964

> switch("e", a=1, b=2, c=3, d=4, 25)
[1] 25

> switch("e", a=1, b=2, c=3, d=4)
> mode(switch("e", a=1, b=2, c=3, d=4))
[1] "NULL"
```

The unnamed argument can appear anywhere in the listing except as the first argument. If more than one unnamed argument is entered, then switch() returns an error.

With a character string for the first argument, the subsequent arguments do not have to be assigned a value, only a name. If the character string matches a name without a value, then switch() continues along the listing of the arguments and returns the value of the next argument with a value. If none of the subsequent arguments contain a value, switch returns a NULL object. For example:

```
> switch("b", a=1,b=2,c=,d=,e=5)
[1] 2

> switch("b", a=1, b=, c=3, d=)
[1] 3

> switch("b", a=1, b=, c=, d=)
> mode(switch("b", a=1, b=, c=, d=))
[1] "NULL"
```

Note that the first argument is enclosed in quotes, while the names of the subsequent arguments are not. The switch() function can be nested.

You can find more information about switch() by entering **?switch** at the R prompt.

PART 6

■ ■ ■

Some Common Functions, Packages, and Techniques

This final part of the book discusses some common functions and describes what is in the packages **base, stats,** and **graphics,** as well as giving brief descriptions of the packages **datasets, grDevices,** and **utils.** It also covers some common frustrations with R and provides solutions. It briefly discusses the class formula and recursive functions.

Chapter 15 goes over some functions for making nice output and for summarizing data textually and visually.

Chapter 16 lists some of the contents of **base, stats,** and **graphics** along with descriptions.

Chapter 17 talks about a number of frustrations that come up often in R and offers solutions. It also describes the class formula and a recursive function.

Some Common Functions, Packages and Techniques

CHAPTER 15

■ ■ ■

Some Common Functions

This chapter covers some common functions in R. The first section discusses the function options(), which sets the default options for R. The second section describes the functions round(), signif(), and noquote(), which are used in formatting objects. The third section covers the function cat(), which is used to print results to the console, a file, or a connection. The fourth section discusses the functions format(), print(), plot(), and summary() for displaying objects. The functions in the fourth section operate differently on different classes of objects. In the fifth section, we cover the functions anova(), coef(), effects(), residuals(), fitted(), vcov(), confint(), and predict(), which are functions that operate specifically on models and which also operate differently depending on the class of the object.

The Function options()

Currently on my Windows system, there are 55 options in the function options(). The options are loaded when the packages are loaded. To see a list of the options with their set values, enter **options()** at the R prompt. The options for all loaded packages are in the list.

To see the value(s) of specific options, enter **options("opt1", "opt2", ... ,"opt_n")** at the R prompt, where **opt1** through **opt_n** are the names of the options. To access the value(s) of an option, use **getOption("opt")**, where **opt** is the name of the option.

To set option values, enter **options(opt1=value1, opt2=value2, opt3=value3, ... , opt_n=value_n)** at the R prompt, where **opt1** through **opt_n** are the options and **value1** through **value_n** are the values assigned to the options. Note that for setting and accessing an option, the option is entered as a character string (in quotes), whereas for setting a value, the option is entered as an object (no quotes).

For descriptions of the options and the packages to which they belong, enter **?options** at the R prompt.

When options are changed during an R session, the change is only good for the session. To change the values of the option defaults that are loaded when R is run, try creating the file .Rprofile in the same folder as .RData and .Rhistory. If the file does not already exist, this method works. If the file does exist, editing the file works. The file .Rprofile must be a plain text file with no extension. The file tells R what functions to run at startup.

Putting lines in the file to run `options()` sets default options. For example, the contents of `.Rprofile` might be the following:

```
options(defaultPackages=c(getOption("defaultPackages"),"MASS"),
contrasts=c("contr.sum","contr.poly"))
```

Here the package **MASS** is added to the packages that are loaded at startup and the contrast for unordered factors is changed from the default "contr.treatment" to "contr.sum". More about the startup process can be found by entering **?Startup** at the R prompt.

Some options include the following:

> `continue`—a character string—gives what R prints at the console when more than one line is used for R code—the default value is `"+"`.

> `contrasts`—character strings—the types of contrasts to use for factor data in linear models—the default values are "contr.treatment" for unordered contrasts and "contr.poly" for ordered contrasts—other possible values are "contr.sum" and "contr.helmert"—information about the contrasts can be found by entering **?contrasts** at the R prompt.

> `defaultPackages`—character strings—the packages to be loaded by default when R is run—the default values are "datasets", "utils", "grDevices", "graphics", "stats", and "methods" (base is always loaded).

> `digits`—an integer—the recommendation for the number of digits to be returned for numbers—R does not necessarily use the recommended number—the default value is "7".

> `editor`—a character string—gives the editor that the function `edit()` calls—the default value varies with operating system—see the help page for `edit()` for more information.

> `expressions`—an integer—how deep nesting can go—the value can be between 25 and 500,000—the default value is "5000".

> `na.action`—a character string giving a function—gives the option for missing values—the default value is "na.omit"—other values are "na.fail", "na.pass", and "na.exclude"—see the help pages for `na.omit()`, `na.fail()`, `na.pass()`, and `na.exclude()` for more information.

> `scipen`—an integer—an option that gives R a tendency toward either scientific notation (negative integers) or fixed notation (positive integers)—see the `options()` help page for more information—the default value is "0".

show.coef.Pvalues—a logical value—an option that tells R whether to show p values in the summary() output from linear models—the default value is "TRUE".

show.signif.stars—a logical value—an option that tells R whether to show stars to give significance levels in the summary() output from linear models—the default value is "TRUE".

stringsAsFactor—a logical value—tells data.frame() and read.table() whether to convert character strings to factors—the default value is "TRUE"—yes convert strings.

OutDec—a single character string—gives the value to use for a decimal point—the default value is ".".

prompt—a character string—the value to use as the R prompt—the default value is ">".

ts.eps—a numeric value—the tolerance level for comparing time periods in more than one time series—the default value is "1.0e-5".

The Functions round(), signif(), and noquote()

The functions round(), signif(), and noquote() make output easier to read.

The Function round()

The function round() rounds the elements of objects of mode numeric or complex to a given number of digits after the decimal point. The function takes two arguments, the object to be rounded, **x**, and the number of digits, **digits**. A negative number for digits rounds to places to the left of the decimal point. For example:

```
> round(c(1.2344, 5.67, 1234.567),3)
[1]    1.234    5.670 1234.567

> round(rnorm(3)+63, -1)
[1] 60 60 60

> round(1.34+3.0i,1)
[1] 1.3+3i
```

Note that all of the values returned have the same number of places after the decimal point, if there is one, except that the real and imaginary parts of complex numbers are treated separately. The default value for **digits** is zero. See the help page of round() for rounding rules if the last digit in **x** equals five.

The Function signif()

The function signif() rounds the elements of a numeric or complex object to a given number of significant digits. The function takes two arguments, the object **x** and the number of significant digits **digit**. For example:

```
> signif(c(1.2344, 5.67, 1234.567),3)
[1]    1.23    5.67 1230.00

> signif(rnorm(3)+63,-1)
[1] 60 60 60

> signif(1.34+3.0i,1)
[1] 1+3i
```

Note that, like round(), all of the returned numbers go out to the same number of places, but the significant digits are limited to the integer given by **digit**. If a value less than one is given for **digit**, then the number of significant digits is set to one. The default value for **digit** is six.

The Function noquote()

The function noquote() returns output where the quotes have been removed from any character strings in the object. The function takes one argument **obj**, which can be any type of object. For example:

```
> noquote(c(" a", "bc", "d"))
[1]    a bc d
```

More information about round() and signif() can be found by entering **?signif** at the R prompt. More information about noquote() can be found by entering **?noquote** at the R prompt.

The Function cat()

The function cat() can be used to output data from a function to the console, a file, or a connection. The function name **cat** stands for *concatenate*. The objects to be concatenated must be of mode atomic and separated by commas. The objects are coerced to vectors. The function has five arguments other than the objects to be concatenated.

The five arguments are **file, sep, fill, labels,** and **append**. The argument **file** tells cat() where to send the output. The argument is a character string and can be a file address, a connection, or ""—for the console. The default value is "". The argument **sep** is a character string. The value of **sep** separates the objects printed in the output. The default value is " ".

The argument **fill** is either a logical variable or a positive number. If **FALSE**, line breaks are set with "\n" or a break in a quoted string. If **TRUE**, the value of the option **width** is used to set the width of the output. If **fill** is a positive number, the number is used to set the width. The default value is **FALSE**.

The argument **labels** is a vector of character strings that is used to label the lines of output and is only used if **fill** is **TRUE** or numeric. The default value is **NULL**. The argument **append** is used when **file** is an external file. If **TRUE**, then the output is appended to the file. Otherwise, the file is overwritten. The default value is **FALSE**.

The string "\n" tells cat() to go to the next line. A line break can also be entered by breaking the line within a quoted string. For example:

```
> set.seed(69235)
> x=1:4
> y= runif(4)
> a.lm=lm(y~x)
> a.sm=summary(a.lm)

> cat("\nThe intercept is ", round(coef(a.lm)[1],3), ". The slope is ",
round(coef(a.lm)[2],3), ".  The F statistic is ", round(a.sm$f[1],4), " on
", a.sm$f[2], " and ", a.sm$f[3], " degrees of freedom.  The p value is ",
round(1-pf(a.sm$f[1], a.sm$f[2], a.sm$f[3]),4), ".\n", sep="")

The intercept is -0.301. The slope is 0.257.  The F statistic is 4.5039 on 1
and 2 degrees of freedom.  The p value is 0.167

> cat(round(coef(a.lm)[1],3), round(coef(a.lm)[2],3), round(a.sm$f[1],4),
a.sm$f[2], a.sm$f[3],
+ round(1-pf(a.sm$f[1], a.sm$f[2], a.sm$f[3]), 3), fill=17, labels =
c("intercept ", "slope       ",
+ "F          ", "df 1 & 2  ", "p value    "))
intercept   -0.301
slope        0.257
F            4.5039
df 1 & 2    1 2
p value      0.168
```

More information about cat() can be found by entering **?cat** at the R prompt.

The Functions format(), print(), plot(), and summary()

The functions format(), print(), plot(), and summary() behave differently depending on the class of the object on which the functions operate. For a given function, in order to see the classes of objects that have special methods for the function, enter **methods('function')** at the R prompt, where **function** is the name of the function.

R automatically uses the special method for an object if the class of the object has a special function, even if the class extension is not included. For example, plot(a.ts) and plot.ts(a.ts) give the same result if a.ts is a time series. If there is no special function for the class of the object, then the default method is used, if there is a default method. For information about the default method, enter **?function.default** at the R prompt, where **function** is the name of the function; for example, ?plot.default.

The Function format()

The function format() has 59 methods on my Windows system, including default. The function returns a character version of atomic objects and, for many list objects, reduced character versions of the list. The function takes several arguments that can structure the output to make a visually nice result. The arguments vary from method to method. For example:

```
> a.date = as.Date(1:4, "2014-3-9")

> a.date
[1] "2014-03-10" "2014-03-11" "2014-03-12" "2014-03-13"

> format(a.date, "%m/%d/%Y")
[1] "03/10/2014" "03/11/2014" "03/12/2014" "03/13/2014"

> a.list = list(c("a","b","c"), matrix(1:4,2,2))

> dimnames(a.list[[2]]) = list(c("r1","r2"),c("c1","c2"))

> a.list
[[1]]
[1] "a" "b" "c"

[[2]]
   c1 c2
r1  1  3
r2  2  4

> format(a.list)
[1] "a, b, c"    "1, 2, 3, 4"
```

For more information about format(), enter **?format** or **?format.'ext'** at the R prompt, where **ext** is the extension for the class. Extensions can be found by entering **methods(format)** at the R prompt.

The Function print()

The function print() prints objects. The function has 201 methods on my Windows system, including default. The functions can take on a variety of arguments depending on the class of the object to be printed. Some useful ones that are available for many classes are **quote**, which is a logical argument that tells print whether to print quotes or not; **print.gap**, which is an integer argument that tells print() how many spaces to put between columns for matrices, arrays, and data frames; and **right**, which is a logical argument that tells print whether to right or left justify strings. For example:

```
> a.mat = matrix(paste("m",1:8,sep=""),2,4)

> print(a.mat)
     [,1] [,2] [,3] [,4]
[1,] "m1" "m3" "m5" "m7"
[2,] "m2" "m4" "m6" "m8"

> print(a.mat, quote=F, right=T, print.gap=3)
      [,1]    [,2]    [,3]    [,4]
[1,]   m1      m3      m5      m7
[2,]   m2      m4      m6      m8
```

To find more information about print() and the various print methods, enter at the R prompt **?print** or **?print.'ext'** where **ext** is the extension for the class of the object.

The Function plot()

The function plot() is one of the functions that makes plots. The function has 33 methods on my Windows system, including default. Plotting in R can go from simple descriptive plots to very sophisticated plots. The subject deserves a book of its own; consequently, it will not be covered here. Information about plot() can be found by entering **?plot** or **?plot.'ext'**, where **ext** is the extension for the class of the object to be plotted.

The Function summary()

The function summary() has 36 methods on my Windows system, including default. For some objects, for example, the output from lm(), summary() is sub-scriptable and returns variables not returnable from the object itself. Some examples follow:

```
> x = sample(3,1000, rep=T)
> y = sample(5,1000, rep=T)

> a.tab = table(x,y)
> a.tab
   y
```

```
x    1  2  3  4  5
   1 69 70 57 59 55
   2 61 78 68 69 68
   3 75 60 72 76 63

> summary(a.tab)
Number of cases in table: 1000
Number of factors: 2
Test for independence of all factors:
        Chisq = 6.641, df = 8, p-value = 0.5758

> a.ar = array(1:8, c(2,2,2))
> a.ar
, , 1

      [,1] [,2]
[1,]    1    3
[2,]    2    4

, , 2

      [,1] [,2]
[1,]    5    7
[2,]    6    8

> summary(a.ar)
   Min. 1st Qu.  Median   Mean 3rd Qu.    Max.
   1.00    2.75    4.50    4.50    6.25    8.00
```

More information about summary( ) can be found by entering **?summary** or **?summary.'ext'**, where **ext** is the extension for the class of the object, at the R prompt.

Some Functions for Models: anova(), coef(), effects(), residuals(), fitted(), vcov(), confint(), and predict()

While print( ), plot( ), and summary( ) have special methods for model classes such as **lm** and **glm**, the functions also cover many other classes. The functions anova( ), coef( ), effects( ), residuals( ), fitted( ), vcov( ), confint( ), and predict( ) are functions which also behave differently depending on the class of the main argument and which are specifically written for models.

For the examples in this section, we use the following liner model:

```
> x=1:5
> y = rnorm(5)
> a.lm = lm(y~x)
```

The function anova() has ten methods on my Windows system and returns an anova table for a model. For example:

```
> anova(a.lm)
Analysis of Variance Table

Response: y
          Df  Sum Sq Mean Sq F value  Pr(>F)
x          1 1.12231 1.12231  7.9294 0.06696 .
Residuals  3 0.42462 0.14154
---
Signif. codes:  0 '***' 0.001 '**' 0.01 '*' 0.05 '.' 0.1 ' ' 1
```

The function coef() has nine methods on my Windows system, including default, and returns the coefficients of a model. For example:

```
> coef(a.lm)
(Intercept)           x
  1.8579552  -0.3350095
```

The function effects() has two methods (**lm** and **glm**) on my Windows system. For example:

```
> effects(a.lm)
(Intercept)                x
 -1.9072023  -1.0593929  -0.1839281  -0.1798352   0.5987044
attr(,"assign")
[1] 0 1
attr(,"class")
[1] "coef"
```

Enter **?effects** at the R prompt for more information about effects().

The function residuals() has nine methods on my Windows system, including default. The function returns the residuals of a model. For example:

```
> residuals(a.lm)
          1           2           3           4           5
-0.04429571  0.35401363 -0.26173492 -0.36138822  0.31340522
```

The function fitted() has six methods on my Windows system, including default, and returns the fitted values for a model. For example:

```
> fitted(a.lm)
        1         2         3         4         5
1.5229457 1.1879363 0.8529268 0.5179174 0.1829079
```

The function vcov( ) has 11 methods on my Windows system and returns the estimated variance-covariance matrix of the coefficients of the model. For example:

```
> vcov(a.lm)
            (Intercept)          x
(Intercept)  0.15569297 -0.04246172
x           -0.04246172  0.01415391
```

The function confint( ) has eight methods on my Windows system, including default. The function returns confidence intervals for the coefficients of a model. For example:

```
> confint(a.lm)
                 2.5 %      97.5 %
(Intercept)  0.6022272  3.11368324
x           -0.7136257  0.04360679
```

The function predict( ) has 23 methods on my Windows system and returns predictions from the model. For some classes of objects, predict( ) can return confidence or prediction intervals for predicted values. If the original model is used for the first argument in predict( ), then the intervals are for the fitted values. For our model **a.lm** and for finding 95-percent confidence intervals for the fitted values, an example follows:

```
> predict(a.lm, interval="confidence")
        fit        lwr      upr
1 1.5229457  0.5955291 2.450362
2 1.1879363  0.5321537 1.843719
3 0.8529268  0.3174826 1.388371
4 0.5179174 -0.1378652 1.173700
5 0.1829079 -0.7445087 1.110325
```

More information for the functions in this section can be found by **entering** **?'function'** or **?'function'.'ext'** at the R prompt, where **function** is the function name and **ext** is the extension for the class.

■ ■ ■

CHAPTER 16

The Packages base, stats, and graphics

In this chapter, we take a quick look at the packages base, stats, and graphics—three of the packages loaded by default in R. The package base contains things such as the trigonometric function and other mathematical functions, many of the **as.** and **is.** functions, the arithmetic operators, the flow control statements, some apply functions, and many other basic functions in R.

The package stats contains many basic statistical functions, such as functions to find the median, the standard deviation, and the variance. It also includes the functions associated with common probability distributions as well as many more. The package graphics contains the basic plotting functions and their ancillary functions.

The other packages loaded by default are datasets, which contains data sets; utils, which contains utility functions; grDevices, which contains information used in plotting—such as fonts and colors; and methods—enter **?Methods** at the R prompt for information about the methods package and about using methods in R.

For a list of the functions in a package with clickable links to the function help pages, enter **help(package=package.name)** at the R prompt, where **package.name** is the name of the package. For information about the package and a text list of the contents of the package, enter **library(help=package.name)** where **package.name** is the name of the package.

The source of the information in this chapter is the CRAN help pages.

The base Package

The base package contains many functions basic to R. The documentation for base is seven pages long (library(help=base)). The list of links to the help pages for base is 32 pages long (help(package=base)). This section covers the reserved words, the built-in constants, the trigonometric and hyperbolic functions, the functions related to the beta and gamma functions, some other mathematical functions, and functions for complex numbers, matrix functions, and a few other functions. It also discusses some other functions for the package base.

Reserved Words

The reserved words in R are **if, else, repeat, while, for, function, next, break, in, TRUE, FALSE, Inf, NULL, NA, NaN, NA_integer_, NA_real_, NA_complex_, NA_character_**, ..., **..1, ..2**, and so forth. See Table 16-1.

Table 16-1. *The Reserved Words in R*

if	else	repeat	while	for
in	next	break	function	TRUE
FALSE	Inf	NULL	NA	NAN
NA_integer_	NA_real_	NA_complex_	NA_character_	
'..'	'.._1'	'.._2'	....	'.._n'

For more information, enter **?Reserved** at the R prompt.

Built-In Constants

The built-in constants in R are **LETTERS**, which are the 26 letters in the English alphabet and which are capitalized; **letters**, which are the 26 letters in the English alphabet and which are lowercase; **month.abb**, which are three-letter abbreviations of the names of the months in English; **month.name**, which are the names of the months in English; and **pi**, the mathematical constant π. See Table 16-2 for a listing of the constants.

Table 16-2. *The Built-In Constants in R*

Constants	Description
LETTERS	the 26 capital letters
letters	the 26 lowercase letters
month.abb	the 12 names of the months abbreviated to three letters
month.name	the 12 names of the months
pi	π; 1/2 the circumference of a unit circle

You can find more information about the constants by entering **?Constants** at the R prompt.

Trigonometric and Hyperbolic Functions

The trigonometric and hyperbolic functions available in R are the cosine - cos(), sine - sin(), tangent - tan(), inverse cosine - acos(), inverse sine - asin(), two versions of the inverse tangent - atan() and atan2(), hyperbolic cosine - cosh(), hyperbolic sine - sinh(), hyperbolic tangent - tanh(), inverse hyperbolic cosine - acosh(), inverse hyperbolic sine - asinh(), and inverse hyperbolic tangent - atanh().

Angles are entered into the functions as radians (radians = pi/180 x degrees). For the inverse functions, the angles are returned in radians (degrees = 180/pi x radians). The arguments must be of an atomic mode and logical, numeric, or complex. Logical values are coerced to numeric.

For the inverse cosine and sine, the values must be between -1 and 1, inclusive. For other values, the result is **NaN**. For the inverse tangent, atan() takes one argument and the result falls between $-\pi/2$ and $\pi/2$.

The function atan2() takes two arguments. The function returns the inverse tangent of the ratio of the two arguments, with the first argument being the numerator and the second the denominator. The function takes any number (real or complex) for the numerator and any number (real or complex) as the denominator. The arguments can be of different lengths and will cycle.

The function atan2() returns results between $-\pi$ and π. The quadrant of the angle depends on signs of the numerator and the denominator, that is: (+,+) first quadrant; (+,-) second quadrant; (-,-) third quadrant; and (-,+) fourth quadrant. (By definition, the tangent of x, for any number x, is the sine of x divided by the cosine of x.) Zero in the denominator returns $\pi/2$ or $-\pi/2$ depending on the sign of the numerator.

The hyperbolic functions can also take on any number (real or complex). For the inverse of the hyperbolic functions, the argument for acosh() must be between 1 and ∞, inclusive, and the argument for atanh() must be between -1 and 1, inclusive.

Arguments can be vectors, matrices, data frames, or arrays. For arguments with more than one element, the operation is carried out element-wise. For atan2(), which takes two arguments, the arguments cycle. The functions return an object of the same dimensions as the argument(s) to the function.

See Table 16-3 for a listing of the functions, with restrictions.

Table 16-3. *The Trigometric and Hyperbolic Functions*

Function	R Function	Restrictions
cosine	cos(x)	logical, numeric, or complex; logical coerced to numeric
sine	sin(x)	see cosine
tangent	tan(x)	see cosine
inverse cosine	acos(x)	$-1 \le x \le 1$
inverse sine	asin(x)	see inverse cosine
inverse tangent	atan(x)	see cosine
""	atan2(y,x)	see cosine; inverse of tangent of **y** divided by **x**; maintains quadrant information

(continued)

Table 16-3. (*continued*)

Function	R Function	Restrictions
hyperbolic cosine	cosh(x)	see cosine
hyperbolic sine	sinh(x)	see cosine
hyperbolic tangent	tanh(x)	see cosine
inverse hyperbolic cosine	acosh(x)	$1 \leq x \leq \infty$
inverse hyperbolic sine	asinh(x)	see cosine
inverse hyperbolic tangent	atanh(x)	$-1 \leq x \leq 1$

You can find more information about the trigonometric functions by entering **?Trig** at the R prompt; for the hyperbolic functions, by entering **?cosh** at the R prompt.

Beta- and Gamma-Related Functions

The functions related to the beta and gamma functions are beta(), lbeta(), gamma(), lgamma(), psigamma(), bigamma(), trigamma(), choose(), lchoose(), factorial(), and lfactorial(). In R, these functions are the **Special** functions. The arguments to these functions must be of the atomic mode and logical (which are coerced to numeric) or numeric. The function returns a result in the same form as the argument (the same dimensions). Arguments cycle.

The beta() and lbeta() functions take the arguments **a** and **b**, both of which must be non-negative, and return the value of the beta function or the natural logarithm of the value of the beta function respectively. Negative numbers return **NaN**.

The gamma(), lgamma(), psigamma(), digamma(), and trigamma() functions take the argument **x**, and for psigamma(), the argument **deriv**. The argument **x** can be any number, except for zero or the negative integers, for which **NaNs** are returned. The functions gamma() and lgamma() return the value of the gamma function and the natural logarithm of the absolute value of the gamma function respectively. The function psigamma() returns the derivative of the natural logarithm of the gamma function to the order given by **deriv**. The argument **deriv** must be an integer greater than or equal to zero. By default, **deriv**, equals zero. The function digamma() returns the value of the first derivative of the natural logarithm of the gamma function while trigamma() returns the second derivative.

The functions choose() and lchoose() return binomial coefficients and the natural logarithms of the absolute values of binomial coefficients, respectively. Both functions take the arguments **n**, which can be any real number, and **k**, which can be any real number and is rounded to an integer. Negative numbers for **k** return **0**. The function choose() is the familiar "**n** choose **k**" for **n** a positive integer and **k** a non-negative integer less than or equal to **n**.

The functions `factorial()` and `lfactorial()` return the factorial value and the natural logarithm of the absolute value of the factorial value, respectively. The functions take one argument, **x**. The value of **x** can be any real number (numeric or logical coerced to numeric). The factorial value is defined as

```
factorial(x) = gamma(x+1)
```

for any value of **x** and equals x! (that is, (x)(x-1)(x-2)...(2)(1)) for positive integer values of **x**. For **x** equal to zero, factorial(x) equals one. Negative integers return NaNs.

See Table 16-4 for a listing of the functions. You can find more information about the functions by entering **?Special** at the R prompt.

Table 16-4. *The Beta, Gamma, and Related Functions*

Function	Function in R	Arguments
beta	beta(a, b)	a, b; both integers ≥ 0
natural log beta	lbeta(a,b)	see beta
gamma	gamma(x)	x, any real number; zero and negative integers return NaN
natural log of absolute value of gamma	lgamma(x)	x, any real number; zero and negative integers return Inf
nth derivative of natural log of gamma function where **deriv** equals **n**	psigamma(x, deriv=0)	x, any real number; deriv, an integer ≥ 0; returns NaN's where not defined
1st derivative of natural log of gamma function	digamma(x)	x, any real number; returns NaN's where not defined
2nd derivative of natural log of gamma function	trigamma(x)	see digamma
binomial coefficients	choose(n, k)	n, any real number k, integer ≥ 0
natural log absolute value binomial coefficients	lchoose(n, k)	see binomial coefficients
factorial	factorial(x)	x, any real number; factorial(x) equals gamma(x+1); negative integers return NaN
natural log absolute value factorial	lfactorial(x)	x, any real number; lfactorial(x) equals lgamma(x+1); negative integers return Inf

Miscellaneous Mathematical Functions

Some other mathematical functions include the following:

abs() for the absolute values of the elements of an object

sqrt() for the square roots of the elements of an object

ceiling() for rounding the elements of an object up to an integer

floor() for rounding the elements of an object down to an integer

trunc() for truncating the elements of an object to the decimal point

cummax() for the cumulative maximum over an atomic object

cummin() for the cumulative minimum over an atomic object

cumprod() for the cumulative product over an atomic object

cumsum() for the cumulative sum over an atomic object

exp() for e to the powers of the elements of an object

log(), log10(), and log2() for the logarithms of the elements of an object for a specified base, base 10, and base 2, respectively

max() for the maximum of the elements in an object

min() for the minimum of the elements in an object

pmax() for vectors (will cycle) or matrices—returns the maximum across rows

pmin() for vectors (will cycle) or matrices—returns the minimum across rows

sum() for the sum of the elements of an object

prod() for the product of the elements of an object

mean() for the mean of the elements of an object

range() for the range of the elements of an object

rank() for the ranks of the elements of an object

sign() for the signs of the elements of an object—returns 1 for positive numbers, -1 for negative numbers, and 0 for zeroes

order() for indices giving the order of the elements of an object; with more than one object, the order of the first object, using the second object for ties, and so forth; used to reorder vectors, matrices, data frames, and arrays; x[order(x)] equals sort(x)

sort() for sorting the elements of objects

zapsmall() for setting very small numbers to zero

Atomic vectors, matrices, arrays, and data frames of the legal modes can be used for these functions. The results of these functions are various types of objects, depending on the function.

See Table 16-5 for a listing of the functions with restrictions.

Table 16-5. *Some Other Mathematical Functions*

Function in R	Restrictions
abs(x)	logical, numeric, or complex objects; logical coerced to numeric; returns object of same dimensions
sqrt(x)	see abs(); negative real numbers return NaN
ceiling(x)	logical or numeric object; logical coerced to numeric; returns object of same dimensions
floor(x)	see ceiling()
trunc(x, ...)	x, logical or numeric object; logical coerced to numeric; returns object of same dimensions
	..., any arguments to be passed on to lower level functions called by trunc()
cummax(x)	raw, logical, numeric, or character object; will be coerced to numeric; character objects return NAs; returns vector
cummin(x)	see cummax()
cumsum(x)	see cummax()
cumprod(x)	see cummax()
exp(x)	logical, numeric, or complex object; logical coerced to numeric; returns object of same dimensions
log(x, base=exp(1))	x, logical, numeric, or complex object; logical coerced to numeric; $x \geq 0$; 0's return -Inf; negative real numbers return NaN; returns object of same dimensions
	base, the base for the logarithm; numeric or complex—logical is legal but returns Inf for T and 0 for F; base ≥ 0
log2(x)	logical, numeric, or complex; logical coerced to numeric; $x \geq 0$; 0's return -Inf; negative real numbers return NaN; returns object of same dimensions
log10(x)	see log2()

(continued)

Table 16-5. (*continued*)

Function in R	Restrictions
max(..., na.rm=FALSE)	..., logical, numeric, complex, and character objects separated by commas; do not need to be of the same length; can mix modes; returns a single value
	na.rm, logical; if an NA is present and na.rm is set to FALSE returns NA, if TRUE ignores the NA
min(..., na.rm=FALSE)	see max()
pmax(..., na.rm=FALSE)	..., logical, numeric, and character objects separated by commas; do not need to be of the same length—cycle; can mix modes; returns a vector
	na.rm, logical; if an NA is present and na.rm is set to FALSE returns NA, if TRUE ignores the NA
pmin(..., na.rm=FALSE)	see pmax()
sum(..., na.rm=FALSE)	..., logical, numeric, and complex objects separated by commas; can mix modes; returns a single value
	na.rm, logical; if an NA is present and na.rm is set to FALSE returns NA, if TRUE ignores the NA; NaN similar but are treated differently for complex numbers
prod(..., na.rm=FALSE)	see sum()
mean(x, trim=0, na.rm=FALSE, ...)	x, logical, numeric, or complex object; returns a single value
	trim, $0 \leq \text{trim} \leq .5$; is proportion of elements to trim before taking the mean
	na.rm, logical; if an NA is present and na.rm is FALSE returns NA, if TRUE ignores NA; NaN the same
	... any arguments to be passed to lower level functions called by mean()
range(..., na.rm=FALSE)	..., logical, numeric, and character objects separated by commas; can mix modes; returns two values
	na.rm, logical; if an NA is present and na.rm is set to FALSE returns NA, if TRUE ignores the NA; NaN the same

(*continued*)

Table 16-5. (continued)

Function in R	Restrictions
rank(x, na.last=TRUE, ties. method=c("average", "first", "random", "max", "min"))	x, logical, numeric, complex, or character object na.last, logical or character; if TRUE, NAs and NaNs are ranked last, if FALSE they are first, if NA they are discarded, if "keep" they keep their place in the order; NaNs return NAs; returns a vector ties.method, character; method for setting a value for ties; the default is "average"
sign(x)	logical or numeric object; returns object of same dimensions
order(..., na.last=TRUE, decreasing=FALSE)	..., logical, numeric, complex or character vectors of the same length—can use just one vector—can mix modes; returns a permutation of indices of length equal to the length of the vector(s) na.last, logical; for TRUE NAs are placed last, for FALSE NAs first, for NA NAs are removed decreasing, logical; must be TRUE or FALSE; if TRUE order is decreasing, if FALSE increasing
sort(x, decreasing=FALSE, na.last=NA, ...)	x, logical, numeric, complex, or character object; sorts real and imaginary parts of complex separately; returns a vector decreasing, logical; if TRUE sorts in decreasing order, if FALSE increasing; must be TRUE or FALSE na.last, logical; if TRUE, NAs are put last, if FASLE, they are put first, if NA they are discarded; NaNs are put last ..., any arguments to be passed on to lower level functions called by sort()
zapsmall(x, digits= getOptions("digits"))	x, logical, numeric, or complex object; returns object of same dimensions digits, numeric; will round to an integer

You can find more information about any of these functions by going to the help page of the function (?**function.name**, where **function.name** is the name of the function).

Complex Numbers

The following functions are for complex numbers:

Re(), the real part of a complex number

Img(), the complex part of a complex number

Arg(), the angle from the x axis in radians of the line between the origin and the complex number

Mod(), the modulus of a complex number; equals the length of the line between the origin and the complex number

Conj(), the complex conjugate of a complex number

The functions take logical, numeric, and complex objects for arguments. Logical arguments are coerced to numeric. The result has the same dimensions as the argument.

You can find more information about the complex functions by entering **?Re** at the R prompt.

Matrices, Arrays, and Data Frames

There is an operator and there are a number of functions for matrices, arrays, and data frames in base that we have not yet covered.

The operator is %x% for the Kronecker product of matrices and arrays. Some of the functions include the following:

aperm(), which permutes an array

rowsum(), which sums over rows of a matrix or data frame in groups set by the **group** variable

colMeans(), which returns the means of the columns of a data frame or matrix or the means for given dimensions for an array—going from the first dimension to the specified dimension

colSums(), which returns the sums of the columns of a data frame or matrix or the sums for an array—going from the first dimension to the specified dimension

rowMeans(), which returns the means of the rows of a data frame or matrix or the sums over dimensions of an array—going from the specified dimension plus one to the last dimension

rowSums(), which returns the sums of the rows or a data frame or matrix—going from the specified dimension plus one to the last dimension

col(), which returns a matrix of the same dimensions as the argument and which contains the column indices in the columns or a matrix of factors with each column one factor

row(), which returns a matrix of the same dimensions as the argument and which contains the row indices in the rows or a matrix of factors with each row one factor

det(), which returns the determinant of a matrix

determinant(), which returns the modulus or the logarithm of the modulus of the determinant and the sign of the modulus

eigen(), which returns the eigenvalues and eigenvectors of a matrix

kappa(), which calculates the condition of a square matrix

kronecker(), which returns the matrix or array which is the kronecker **product** of two objects and where **product** is a specified function. The two objects can be vectors, matrices, and/or arrays. The dimensions of the result are the products of the dimensions of the two objects.

norm(), which returns the norm of a matrix calculated by the **one**, **infinity**, **Frobenius**, **maximum modulus**, or **spectral** (or **2** method)

Some functions used in model fitting are the following:

backsolve(), which solves a matrix equation where the matrix on the left of the equation is upper triangular

forwardsolve(), solves a matrix equation where the matrix on the left of the equation is lower triangular

chol(), the Choleski decomposition of a square positive definite matrix

chol2inv(), the inverse of a positive definite matrix using the Choleski decomposition of the matrix

qr(), the QR decomposition of a matrix

svd(), a singular value decomposition of a matrix.

See Table 16-6 for a listing of the functions with arguments.

Table 16-6. *Some Functions for Matrices, Arrays, and Data Frames*

Function in R	Restrictions
aperm(a, perm=NULL, resize=TRUE, ...)	a, matrix or array
	perm, NULL, integer or character vector; gives order of the dimensions by index or character string; if not NULL must be of length equal to the dimensions of **a** and a permutation of the dimensions of **a**; NULL returns the dimensions reversed
	resize, logical; must be TRUE or FALSE
	..., any arguments to be passed to lower level functions
rowsum(x, group, reorder=TRUE, na.rm=FALSE, ...)	x, any numeric matrix
	group, a vector or factor of length equal to the number of rows in x—used for grouping
	reorder, logical; must be TRUE or FALSE
	na.rm, logical; must be TRUE or FALSE
	..., any arguments to be passed to or from lower level functions
colMeans(x, na.rm=FALSE, dims=1)	x, logical, numeric or complex matrix, data frame, or array
	na.rm, logical; must be TRUE or FALSE
	dims, numeric; $1 \leq$ dims $\leq$ n-1, where n is the number of dimensions
colSums(x, na.rm=FALSE, dims=1)	see colMeans()
rowMeans(x, na.rm=FALSE, dims=1)	see colMeans()
rowSums(x, na.rm=FALSE, dims=1)	see colMeans()
col(x, as.factor=FALSE)	x, any matrix
	as.factor, logical; must be TRUE or FALSE
row(x, as.factor=FALSE)	see col()
det(x, ...)	x, a logical or numeric square matrix; logical coerced to numeric
	..., ignored

(continued)

Table 16-6. (*continued*)

Function in R	Restrictions
determinant(x, logarithm=TRUE, ...)	x, a logical or numeric square matrix; logical coerced to numeric
	logarithm, logical; must be TRUE or FALSE
	..., ignored
eigen(x, symmetric, only.values=FALSE, EISPACK=FALSE)	x, a logical, numeric, or complex square matrix; logical coerced to numeric
	symmetric, logical; if TRUE matrix is assumed symmetric, if FALSE not
	only.values, logical; if TRUE only eigenvalues are returned, if FALSE both eigenvalues and eigenvectors are returned
	EISPACK, logical; defunct and ignored
kappa(z, exact=FALSE, norm=NULL, method= c("qr", "direct"), ..)	z, logical or numeric square matrix; logical coerced to numeric
	exact, logical; must be TRUE or FALSE
	norm, character; must be NULL, "O", or "I"—for norm one and norm infinite
	method, character; must be "qr" or "direct"; default is "qr"
	..., any arguments to lower level functions
kronecker(X, Y, FUN="*", make.names=FALSE, ...)	X, Y, vectors, matrices, and arrays; do not have to be of the same mode; must be legal for the function **FUN**
	FUN, a function; can be a character string
	make.names, logical; must be TRUE or FALSE; does not work with all functions
	..., any arguments for the function **FUN**
norm(x, type= c("O","I","F","M", "2")	x, logical, numeric, or complex matrix; logical and complex are coerced to numeric
	type, character; default value is "O"

(*continued*)

Table 16-6. (*continued*)

Function in R	Restrictions
backsolve(r, x, k=ncol(r), upper.tri=TRUE, transpose=FALSE)	r, upper triangular matrix of mode logical, numeric, or complex—logical and complex values are coerced to numeric
	x, vector or matrix of mode logical, numeric, or complex—logical and complex values are coerced to numeric
	k, numeric—rounds down to an integer; $1 \leq k \leq$ ncol(r); is the number of columns in 'r' to use
	upper.tri, logical; for TRUE the upper triangle is used, for FALSE, the lower is used
	transpose, logical; for TRUE **r** is transposed in the formula
forwardsolve(l, x, k=ncol(l), upper.tri=FALSE, transpose=FALSE)	l, lower triangular matrix of mode logical, numeric, or complex—logical and complex values are coerced to numeric
	x, a vector or matrix of mode logical, numeric, or complex—logical and complex values are coerced to numeric
	k, numeric—rounds down to an integer; $1 \leq k \leq$ ncol(l); the number of columns in 'l' to use
	upper.tri, logical; for TRUE the upper triangle is used, for FALSE, the lower is used
	transpose, logical; for TRUE **l** is transposed in the formula
chol(x, pivot=FALSE, LINPACK=FALSE, tol=-1, ...)	x, raw, logical, or numeric matrix—where raw and logical matrices are coerced to numeric; must be square and positive definite
	pivot, logical; for TRUE pivot, FALSE do not pivot
	LINPACK, (deprecated) logical; for TRUE use LINPACK, FALSE do not use LINPACK
	tol, numeric; tolerance when pivot=TRUE and LINPACK=FALSE
	..., any arguments to be passed to lower level functions

(*continued*)

Table 16-6. (*continued*)

Function in R	Restrictions
chol2inv(x, size=NCOL(x), LINPACK=FALSE)	x, matrix for which the first **size** columns are a Choleski decomposition
	size, numeric, logical, or complex - logical and complex coerced to numeric; 1 ≤ size ≤ ncol(x)
	LINPACK, logical; defunct—no longer used
qr(x, tol=1e-7, LAPACK=FALSE, ...)	x, logical, numeric, or complex matrix; logical matrices are coerced to numeric
	tol, numeric; tolerance for singularity
	LAPACK, logical; if FALSE qr() uses LINPACK
	..., any arguments to be passed to lower level functions
svd(x, nu=min(n,p), nv=min(n,p), LINPACK=FALSE)	x, logical, numeric, or complex matrix; logical matrices are coerced to numeric
	nu, integer; 0 ≤ nu ≤ n; n = nrow(x)
	nv, integer; 0 ≤ nv ≤ p; p = ncol(x)
	LINPACK, logical; defunct and ignored

You can find more information by going to the individual help pages (**?function. name**, where **function.name** is the name of the function).

A Few Other Functions and Some Comments

A few other functions that are often useful are unique(), jitter(), append(), duplicated() (and anyDuplicated()), attr() (and attributes()), pretty(), prop. table(), cut(), rev(), and stop(). For the functions, we will just describe what they do. You can find more information about the functions by entering **?'function.name'** at the R prompt, where **function.name** is the name of the function.

Following are the function descriptions:

> unique() returns a vector with any duplicated elements in the original vector removed. The function only works on vectors, including vectors of mode list.

> jitter() adds a little jitter (noise) to the elements of numeric objects. The arguments to jitter() control how much jitter is added.

> append() is used to append vectors. An argument to append() gives where along the vector the appending is done.

duplicated() and anyDuplicated() look for duplicates. For vectors, including lists, duplicated() returns a vector of the same length containing **FALSE** for elements that are not duplicated and for the first instance of elements that are duplicated. The function returns **TRUE** for the rest of the duplicates. For matrices and data frames, rows are compared. The function anyDuplicated() counts how many differing elements have duplicates, or duplicated rows for matrices and data frames.

attr() and attributes() return an attribute or a list of the attributes of an object. To use an attribute, the function attr() returns a value that can be accessed. To see a list of the attributes of an object, use attributes().

pretty() takes any object that can be coerced to numeric and returns a vector of evenly spaced values close to a given length and similar to the values in the original object.

prop.table() takes a logical, numeric, or complex object and returns the object divided by the sum of the elements in the object. Logical objects are coerced to numeric and the real and imaginary parts of complex objects are treated separately.

cut() cuts a numeric vector into factors and returns a character vector with the factor names in the place of the original elements. The object to be cut can be any object that can be coerced to vector, but must be numeric. The break points and factor names can be assigned, but cut() creates break points and factor names from the break points by default.

rev() reverses the order of the elements of an object and returns a vector. The object can be atomic or of any mode where reversing the order makes sense, like the modes list, expression, and call.

stop() tells R to stop the execution of a function. If stop() has a character string for an argument, the character string prints when stop() executes. The function is very useful for the process of debugging a function as well as for checking if conditions are met for objects entered into a function.

There are many other functions in base, many of which have to do with the running of R. The **as.** and **is.** functions are prevalent. In the list of help pages, there are 52 links for **as.** functions and 44 links for **is.** functions. If you are interested in what is in the listings, go to the page of the links and look at what is there. The Bessel functions are also part of base.

The stats Package

The stats package contains items such as basic descriptive statistics, probability distributions, tests, functions to fit models, clustering functions, some plotting functions and other functions used for outputting results. The documentation for stats is six pages long (library(help=stats)). The list of links to the help pages for stats is 18 pages long (help(package=stats)). In this chapter, we cover the basic descriptive statistics, the tests, clustering and other functions for multivariate data, and modeling functions, but in little detail. The probability distributions can be found in Chapter 9.

Basic Descriptive Statistics

Some of the basic statistical functions in package stats include the following:

weighted.mean(), which finds the weighted mean of an object

sd(), which finds the standard deviation of an object

var(), which finds the variance of a vector or the covariance matrix of a matrix or data frame

cov(), which finds the covariance matrix of a matrix or data frame—more flexible than var()

cov.wt(), which finds the weighted covariance or correlation matrix of a matrix or data frame

cor(), which finds the correlation between vectors or within matrices and data frames

median(), which finds the median of the elements of an object

mad(), which finds the median absolute deviation of the elements of an object

IQR(), which finds the interquartile range of the elements of an object

quantile(), which finds specific quantiles of the elements in an object

fivenum(), which finds Tukey's five-number summary for the elements in an object

ave(), which uses a function to operate on different rows of an object

cancor(), which finds the canonical correlation between two matrices

dist(), which finds a type of average difference between the rows of a matrix, based on the type of distance and the power used to find the average

mahalanobis(), which finds the Mahalanobis distance between rows of a matrix

ecdf(), which finds the empirical cumulative distribution function of the elements in an object—a quantile method exists for the function

r2dtable(), which creates a random two-way table based on marginal values—using Patefield's algorithm

simulate(), which simulates observations from a model that has been fitted

TukeyHSD(), which finds confidence intervals for the coefficients of a model that take into account that more than one hypothesis is being tested—for analysis of variance models

xtabs(), which creates a contingency table based on a formula

smooth(), which creates a smoother version of a noisy set of data using Tukey's running median smoothers—usually used for time series

See Table 16-7 for a listing of the functions, with arguments.

Table 16-7. *Basic Statistical Functions in Package* stats

Function in R	Description
weighted.mean(x, w, ..., na.rm=FALSE)	Finds the weighted mean of x, where x is coerced to a vector.
sd(x, na.rm=FALSE)	Finds the standard deviation x, where x is coerced to a vector; divides by the square root of (n-1).
var(x, y=NULL, na.rm=FALSE, use)	Finds the variance of x if x is a vector or the covariance of x and y or the covariance matrix of x if x is a matrix or data frame; divides by (n-1)
cov(x, y=NULL, use="everything", method=c("pearson", "kendall", "spearman"))	Finds the covariance between x and y if y is given or the covariance matrix of x if x is a matrix or data frame; more options are available than with var()
cov.wt(x, wt=rep(1/nrow(x), nrow(x)), cor=FALSE, center=TRUE, method=c("unbiased", "ML"))	Finds the weighted covariance matrix or weighted correlation matrix of x, where x is a matrix or data frame
cor(x, y=NULL, use="everything", method=c("pearson", "kendall", "spearman"))	Finds the correlation between x and y if y is supplied or within x if just x is supplied, where x is a vector, matrix, or data frame

(continued)

Table 16-7. (*continued*)

Function in R	Description
median(x, na.rm=FALSE)	Finds the median of the elements of x
mad(x, center=median(x), constant=1.4826, na.rm=FALSE, low=FALSE, high=FALSE)	Finds the median absolute deviation of x
IQR(x, na.rm=FALSE, type=7)	Finds the interquartile range of x
quantile(x, probs=seq(0,1,.25), na.rm=FALSE, names=TRUE, type=7, ...)	Finds the quantiles of x for the values of probs
fivenum(x, na.rm=FALSE)	Finds Tukey's five-number summary for x
ave(x, ..., FUN=mean)	The function in FUN operates on groups of the elements of x, where the grouping variables are in the argument ...
cancor(x, y, xcenter=TRUE, ycenter=TRUE)	Finds canonical correlation between the matrices x and y
dist(x, method="euclidean", diag=FALSE, upper=FALSE, p=2)	Finds distance between rows of a matrix, where the type of distance is specified by method
mahalanobis(x, center, cov, inverted=FALSE)	Finds the Mahalanobis distance between rows of a matrix
ecdf(x)	Finds the empirical cumulative distribution function of x
r2dtable(n, r, c)	Creates a random table based on marginal totals for the rows and columns
simulate(x, nsim=1, seed=NULL, ...)	Simulates observations from the model given in x; x is a model
TukeyHSD(x, which, order=FALSE, conf.level=0.95, ...)	Tukey's honest significant differences for analysis of variance models
xtabs(formula=~., data=parent.frame(), subset, sparse=FALSE, na.action, exclude=c(NA,NaN), drop.unused. levels=FALSE)	Creates a contingency table based on the formula, where the variables on the right side of the formula are used to group the object on the left
smooth(x, kind=c("3RS3R", "3RSS", "3RSR", "3R", "3S", "3", "S"), twiceit=FALSE, endrule="Tukey", do.ends=FALSE)	Smooths a vector or time series using Tukey's running median smoothers

You can find more information about the functions by entering **? function.name** at the R prompt where **function.name** is the name of the function.

Some Functions That Do Tests

There are a number of functions in stats that do hypothesis tests. Some of the functions include the following:

bartlett.test() for the homogeneity of variances

binomial.test() for exact tests using the binomial distribution

Box.test() for the Box-Pierce and Ljug-Box tests—used in time series to test for independence

chisq.test() for testing count data using Pearson's test

cor.test() for correlations in paired samples

fisher.test() for contingency tables using Fisher's exact test

fligner.test() for the Fligner-Killeen test for homogeneity of variances

friedman.test() for the Friedman rank sum test

kruskal.test() for the Kruskal-Wallis rank sum test

mantelhaen.test() for the Cochran-Mantel-Haenszel chi squared test for count data

mauchly.test() for the test of sphericity developed by Mauchly

mcnemar.test() for the chi squared test for count data developed by McNemar

mood.test() for the two sample tests of scale developed by Mood

oneway.test() for testing for equal means if the layout is one way

pairwise.prop.test() for comparing proportions pairwise

pairwise.t.test() for comparing t tests pairwise

pairwise.wilcox.test() for comparing Wilcox rank sum tests pairwise

poisson.test() for an exact test using the Poisson distribution

power.anova.test() to find powers for a balanced one-way analysis or variance power.prop.test() to find the powers for comparing two proportions

power.t.test() for the powers in one and two sample t tests

PP.test() for the Phillops-Perron test to test for unit roots in time series data

prop.test() for testing proportions

prop.trend.test() for testing trend in proportions

quade.test() for the Quade test

shapiro.test() for the Shapiro-Wilk test for normality

t.test() for doing a t test

var.test() for an F test to compare two variances

wilcox.test() for Wilcoxon rank sum and sign tests

The tests are listed with arguments in Table 16-8.

Table 16-8. *Some Tests in* stats

Test
bartlett.test(x, g, ...)
biniom.test(x, n, p=0.5, alternative=c("two-sided", "less", "greater"), conf.level=0.95)
Box.test(x, lag=1, type=c("Box-Pierce", "Ljung-Box"), fitdf=0)
chisq.test(x, y=NULL, correct=TRUE, p=rep(1/length(x), length(x)), rescale.p=FALSE, B=2000)
cor.test(x, y, alternative=c("two.sided", "less", "greater"), method=c("pearson", "kendall", "spearman"), exact=NULL, conf.level=0.95, continuity=FALSE, ...)
fisher.test(x, y=NULL, workspace=200000, hybrid=FALSE, control=list(), or=1, alternative="two.sided", conf.int=TRUE, conf.level=0.95, simulate.p.value=FALSE, B=2000)
fligner.test(x, g, ...)
friedman.test(y, groups, blocks, ...)
kruskal(x, g, ...)
ks.test(x, y, ..., alternative=c("two-sided", "less", "greater"), exact=NULL)
mantelhaen.test(x, y=NULL, z=NULL, alternative=c("two.sided", "less", "greater"), correct=T, exact=F, conf.level=0.95)

(continued)

Table 16-8. (*continued*)

Test

mauchly.test(object, . . .)

mcnemar.test(x, y=NULL, correct=TRUE)

mood.test(x, y, alternative=c("two.sided", "less", "greater"), . . .)

oneway.test(formula, data, subset, na.action, var.equal=FALSE)

pairwise.prop.test(x, n, p.adjust.method=p.adjust.methods, . . .)

pairwise.t.test(x, g, p.adjust.method=p.adjust.methods, pool.sd=!paired, paired=FALSE, alternative=c("two.sided", "less", "greater"), . . .)

pairwise.wilcox.test(x, g, p.adjust.method=p.adjust.methods, paired=FALSE, . . .)

poisson.test(x, T=1, r=1, alternative=c("two-sided", "less", "greater"), conf.level=0.95)

power.anova.test(groups=NULL, n=NULL, between.var=NULL, within.var=NULL, sig. level=0.05, power=NULL)

power.prop.test(n=NULL, p1=NULL, p2=NULL, sig.level=0.05, power=NULL, alternative=c("two-sided", "one.sided"), strict=FALSE)

power.t.test(n=NULL, delta=NULL, sd=1, sig.level=0.05, type=c("two.sample", "one.sample", "paired"), alternative=c("two.sided", "one.sided"), strict=FALSE)

PP.test(x, lshort=TRUE)

prop.test(x, n, p=NULL, alternative=c("two-sided", "less", "greater"), conf.level=0.95, correct=TRUE)

prop.tend.test(x, n, score=seq_along(x))

quade.test(y, . . .)

shapiro.test(x)

t.test(x, y=NULL, alternative=c("two-sided", "less", "greater"), mu=0, paired=FALSE, var. equal=FALSE, conf.level=0.95, . . .)

var.test(x, y, ratio=1, alternative=c("two-sided", "less", "greater"), conf.level=0.95, . . .)
wilcox.test(x, y=NULL, alternative=c("two-sided", "less", "greater"), mu=0, paired=FALSE, exact=NULL, correct=TRUE, conf.int=FALSE, conf.level=0.95, . . .)

For more information about any of the tests, enter **? function.name** at the R prompt where **function.name** is the name of the function.

Some Modeling Functions in stats

There are a number of functions in stats that do modeling, including the following:

acf() to estimate autocorrelation and autocovariance in time series

aov() to fit an analysis of variance model

ar() to fit a time series autoregressive model

arima() to fit an autoregressive integrated moving average to time series data

ccf() to estimate cross correlation and cross covariance for two time series

cpgram() to plot a cumulative periodogram for time series data

glm() to fit a generalized linear model

fft() for fast discrete fourier transforms for time series data

filter() for linear filtering of time series

KalmanForcast(), KalmanLike(), KalmanRun(), KalmanSmooth(), and makeARIMA() for Kalman filtering

line() to fit a line robustly—based on Tukey's **Exploratory Data Analysis**

lm() to fit a linear model

loess() to fit a local polynomial model

loglin() to fit a loglinear model

lsfit() to fit a least squared linear model with one explanatory variable

manova() to fit multiple analysis of variance models

mvfft() for fast discrete fourier transforms for matrices

nlm() to find a minimum of a nonlinear model

nls() to fit a nonlinear least squares model

optim(), optimHess(), optimise(), and optimize() to optimize a function

pacf() to estimate partial autocovariances and autocorrelations for a time series

ppr() to fit a projection pursuit regression model

smooth.spline() to fit a smooth spline model

spec() to find the spectral density for time series data

step() to use the AIC to choose a model using a stepwise algorithm

stl() to use the loess method to seasonally decompose a time series

StrucTS() to fit a structural time series model

supsmu() for Friedman's super smoother

There are many functions in stats that support the modeling functions, which we do not cover. You can find more information at the help pages for the individual functions: enter **?function.name** at the R prompt where **function.name** is the name of the function.

Clustering Algorithms and Other Multivariate Techniques

Some of the functions used in multivariate analysis for clustering and working with multivariate data are the following:

cmdscal() for classical multidimensional scaling

cophenetic() for cophenetic distances in hierarchical clustering

cut.dendrogram() for a general tree structure

cutree() for cutting a tree into groups

dendrapply() to apply a function to all nodes of a dendrogram

as.dendrogram() to give an appropriate object the class dendrogram

factanal() for factor analysis

hclust() for hierarchical clustering

identify.hclust() to identify clusters

kmeans() for k means clustering

labels.dendrogram() gives the ordering of or the labels of the leaves on a dendrogram

loadings() printing loadings from a factor analysis

merge.dendrogram() merges two dendrograms

order.dendrogram() gives the ordering or the labels of the leaves of a dendrogram

prcomp() does principal components analysis

princomp() also does principal component analysis

promax() used for rotation of axes in factor analysis

reorder.dendrogram() for reordering a dendrogram maintaining the initial constraints

rev.dendrogram() reverses the order of the nodes in a dendrogram

str.dendrogram() displays the internal structure of a dendrogram

varimax() used for rotation of axes in factor analysis

For more information about any of the functions, enter **?'function.name'** at the R prompt where **function.name** is the name of the function.

The package stats also contains several probability distributions (see Chapter 9); eight **as.** functions; six **is.** functions; a number of plotting functions—like heatmap() and 20 **plot.** functions—which are specific for many of the classes associated with modeling functions; functions used in kernel estimation; ancillary functions for models—like the seven **model.** functions; seven **na.** functions—to handle missing data; 14 **predict.**—functions for model output, 36 **print.** functions for printing output; and ten **summary.** functions for summarizing output.

The graphics Package

The package graphics contains the function plot()—for which the many **plot.** methods are written. The ancillary functions for plot() are also in graphics. There are also several plotting functions for specific types of plots—like histograms and bar charts. The documentation for graphics is two pages long (library(help=base)). The list of links to the help pages for base is three pages long (help(package=base)). In this section, we cover the specific types of plots and a few other functions related to plotting.

Following are the functions in graphics that do specific types of plots:

assocplot() for a Cohen-Friendly association plot; used for contingency tables; will work with any matrix that is logical or numeric

barplot() for a bar plot; takes vector or matrix objects, which are of mode logical or numeric, for the heights of the bars

boxplot() for box plots; logical or numeric vectors, matrices, arrays, data frames, and some lists can be used as input to the function

cdplot() for a conditional density plot

coplot() for scatter plots using a conditioning variable

dotchart() for a Cleveland's dot plot; numeric vectors and matrices can be used for the plot hist() for histograms; gives histograms for numeric vectors, matrices, and arrays

mosaicplot() for mosaic plots; takes numeric or logical arguments that are vectors, matrices, data frames, or arrays; is meant for contingency tables

pairs() for scatter plots of paired variables; takes numeric vectors, matrices, and data frames as input; creates a matrix of plots

persp() for a perspective plot; does three-dimensional plotting

pie() for pie charts; use numeric vectors, matrices, and arrays as input

smoothScatter() for a smoothed version of scatter plots—which are colored; is copyrighted by M. P. Wand

spineplot() for spine plots; use a logical, numeric, or complex matrix as input to the plot; logical and complex matrices are coerced to numeric; was developed for two-way contingency tables

stars() for star or segment plots; use a numeric matrix or data frame for the input to the plot

stem() for a stem and leaf plot; use a numeric vector, matrix, or array as the input to the plot

sunflowerplot() for a sunflower plot, which is a scatter plot in which points with duplicates have sunflower leaves for the duplicated points; use a logical, numeric, or complex vector, matrix, or data frame for the input to the plot

There are also some functions in graphics that control the screen for plotting functions. The function splitscreen() and its ancillary functions close.screen(), erase.screen(), and screen() are used to split the plotting screen into regions and to plot to the regions. The functions frame() and plot.new() open a new frame for plotting.

The function par() is like options()—except for plotting—and contains the default options for plots. The options can be changed at any time. Calling par() opens a new plotting frame. To see the list of options, call par() with no arguments.

The function plot() is the basic plotting function and has a numbers of ancillary functions and is defined for quite a few methods. We do not cover plot() in this book.

You can find more information about the functions in graphics by entering **?** **function.name** at the R prompt where **function.name** is the name of the function.

CHAPTER 17

Tricks of the Trade

This book would not be complete without advice on some tricky parts of R. When it seems that everything is set up right, but things still do not do what you expect and you do not know why, this chapter can help. This chapter also describes some not-so-obvious parts of R.

Value Substitution: NA, NaN, Inf, and -Inf

This section has to do with missing data (**NA**) or illegal elements (**NaN, Inf,** or **-Inf**). Say you want to substitute a value, for example **0**, for missing values. The intuitive approach would be to enter something like the following:

```
mat[ mat==NA ] = 0
```

This does not work. What does work is to enter the following:

```
mat [ is.na(mat) ] = 0
```

For example:

```
> mat = matrix(c(1,NA,3,4),2,2)
> mat
     [,1] [,2]
[1,]    1    3
[2,]   NA    4

> mat[ mat==NA ]=2
> mat
     [,1] [,2]
[1,]    1    3
[2,]   NA    4

> mat[ is.na(mat) ]=2
> mat
     [,1] [,2]
[1,]    1    3
[2,]    2    4
```

The same method works for illegal values. The values **NaN**, **Inf**, and **-Inf** are defined in R for illegal operations. For example:

```
> 1/0
[1] Inf

> -1/0
[1] -Inf

> 0/0
[1] NaN

> log(-1)
[1] NaN
Warning message:
In log(-1) : NaNs produced
```

In this example, dividing a positive number by zero results in plus infinity; dividing a negative number by zero gives negative infinity; dividing zero by zero is not defined, so **NaN** is returned. Trying to find the logarithm of minus one returns **NaN** with a warning since the logarithm of minus one is not defined.

The functions is.finite(), is.infinite(), and is.nan() take the place of is.na() in tests for finite, **Inf** and **-Inf**, and **NaN** elements. For example:

```
> mat = matrix(c(1,NaN,Inf,-Inf),2,2)
> mat
     [,1] [,2]
[1,]    1  Inf
[2,]  NaN -Inf

> mat[is.finite(mat)]=2
> mat
     [,1] [,2]
[1,]    2  Inf
[2,]  NaN -Inf

> mat[is.infinite(mat)]=3
> mat
     [,1] [,2]
[1,]    2    3
[2,]  NaN    3

> mat[is.nan(mat)]=4
> mat
     [,1] [,2]
[1,]    2    3
[2,]    4    3
```

Note that is.infinite() treats **Inf** and **-Inf** the same.

The function sign() returns **-1** for an argument equal to **-Inf**. As a result, a simple way to handle the sign problem is to take the sign of the object first, and then multiply the absolute value of the object resulting from the substitution by the sign object after assigning a number to **-Inf**. For example:

```
> mat=matrix(c(1,2,Inf,-Inf),2,2)
> mat
     [,1] [,2]
[1,]    1  Inf
[2,]    2 -Inf

> sg.mat = sign(mat)
> sg.mat
     [,1] [,2]
[1,]    1    1
[2,]    1   -1

> mat[is.infinite(mat)] = 4
> mat
     [,1] [,2]
[1,]    1    4
[2,]    2    4

> mat = sg.mat*abs(mat)
> mat
     [,1] [,2]
[1,]    1    4
[2,]    2   -4
```

You can find more information about **NA** and is.na() by entering **?is.na** at the R prompt. You can find more information about **NaN**, **Inf**, **-Inf**, is.nan(), is.finite(), and is.infinite()by entering **?is.finite** at the R prompt.

If Statements and Logical Vectors

Often when a logical test is done, the objects being tested are of length greater than one. R does not like this and gives a warning that only the first logical element is used. Suppose you want to test whether any element of a logical object is TRUE. Then the function any() is useful. The function any() returns **TRUE** if there are any **TRUE**s in the object, and **FALSE** otherwise. For example:

```
> a.logical=c(T,T,F,T)
> a.logical
[1] TRUE TRUE FALSE TRUE
> test=8
> test
[1] 8
```

```
> if (a.logical==T) test=1
Warning message:
In if (a.logical == T) test = 1 :
  the condition has length > 1 and only the first element will be used
> test
[1] 1

> if (any(a.logical)) test=2
> test
[1] 2

> if (any(!a.logical)) test=3
> test
[1] 3

> if (any(!a.logical[1:2])) test=4
> test
[1] 3
```

Note that in the third and fourth tests, the test is for **FALSE**s. The ! is used to logically negate the object **as.logical** in the test for **FALSE**s.

You can find more information about any( )by entering **?any** at the R prompt.

Lists and the Functions list( ) and c( )

Adding to lists can be confusing. Do you use list( ) or c( )? When creating a list, the elements to be entered into the list are separated by commas. But say you want to add some elements. Then you will usually want to use c( ). For example:

```
> a.list = list(1:4, paste("a",1:7,sep=""))
> a.list
[[1]]
[1] 1 2 3 4

[[2]]
[1] "a1" "a2" "a3" "a4" "a5" "a6" "a7"

> b.list = list(a.list,1:3)
> b.list
[[1]]
[[1]][[1]]
[1] 1 2 3 4

[[1]][[2]]
[1] "a1" "a2" "a3" "a4" "a5" "a6" "a7"
```

```
[[2]]
[1] 1 2 3

> c.list = c(a.list,1:3)
> c.list
[[1]]
[1] 1 2 3 4

[[2]]
[1] "a1" "a2" "a3" "a4" "a5" "a6" "a7"

[[3]]
[1] 1

[[4]]
[1] 2

[[5]]
[1] 3

> d.list = c(a.list,list(1:3))
> d.list
[[1]]
[1] 1 2 3 4

[[2]]
[1] "a1" "a2" "a3" "a4" "a5" "a6" "a7"

[[3]]
[1] 1 2 3
```

The object d.list is probably what you wanted as a result. (Another method to get the same results is to use append() instead of c() in the above expressions.)

Getting Data out of Functions

When you are writing functions, sometimes the purpose of the function is to print results to the console; sometimes the purpose is to export an object—which will be written to the console if not assigned to an object; and sometimes both types of output are needed. The functions print() and cat() write to the console. To output an object, the object must be the last statement in the function. For example:

```
> a.function = function() {
  print(1:3)
  print(5:6)
  }
```

```
> a.function()
[1] 1 2 3
[1] 5 6

> a.result = a.function()
[1] 1 2 3
[1] 5 6

> a.result
[1] 5 6
```

Since the two sequences are in print functions in the example, the sequences are printed out whether an assignment takes place or not. Note that only the second sequence is assigned to the object a.result, since the print statement for the second sequence is the last statement in the function before the close bracket. For another example, the print() function is removed:

```
> a.function = function() {
  1:3
  5:6
  }

> a.function()
[1] 5 6

> a.result = a.function()

> a.result
[1] 5 6
```

In this example, since there is no print() function, the sequences are not printed. The second sequence, being the last statement, is returned by the function.

Recursive Functions

R functions can be applied recursively. A recursive function is a function that calls itself until a condition is met. We use the series that defines the exponential distribution to illustrate the workings of a recursive function.

Recall that

$$e^x = \sum_{i=0}^{\infty} \frac{x^i}{i!}.$$

So, we want a function that adds $\frac{x^i}{i!}$ at each step for i equal to **0, 1, ..., n** for some stopping point **n**. Since $\frac{x^i}{i!}$ decreases at each step and gets arbitrarily small, we used the size of $\frac{x^i}{i!}$ to set the stopping point.

The function follows:

```
> r.exp =
function(x,i=0) {
 if (abs( x^i/factorial(i) ) > 1.0e-8) {

  r.exp(x,i+1) + x^i/factorial(i)

 }
 else {
  0
 }
}
```

At the first step of the recursion, **i** equals zero, so the value of `r.exp()` is

$$r.exp(x,1)+\frac{x^0}{0!}$$

At the second step, the value is

$$r.exp(x,2)+\frac{x^1}{1!}+\frac{x^0}{0!}$$

If **i** equal to **n** is the last step before $x^i/i!$ is less than our stopping point of 1.0e-8, then for **i** equal to **n**, the value of r.exp() equals

$$r.exp(x,n+1)+\sum_{i=0}^{n}\frac{x^i}{i!}$$

But

$$r.exp(x,n+1)=0$$

so the recursion stops. Since the expression in the **if** section of the function is the last statement executed in the function, the function returns the result.

To see how the function works, we let **x** equal one:

```
> r.exp(1)
[1] 2.718282

> exp(1)
[1] 2.718282
```

Note that for **x** equal to one, the function gives the same value as the function exp( ).

Some Final Comments

R is a great program. In this last section, we give some final comments.

First, there is a class that we should have included earlier, the class formula. Formulas such as **y~x** are of class formula and can be assigned a name. Formulas are used in many of the modeling functions or as a way of grouping the object on the left by the values of the objects on the right, for example in boxplot(). In boxplot(), a box plot is created for the values on the left of the tilde for each combination of the values on the right of the tilde.

On the left of the tilde is one object that can be a vector or a matrix and that is the dependent variable(s). On the right of the tilde are the independent variables separated by plus or minus signs. See the help page for formula for information about crossing and nesting variables as well as not including various variables—such as the intercept term or a specific interaction. You can open the help page by entering **?formula** at the R prompt.

R takes some determination to use. If you get stuck on a problem and cannot find an answer, do not be afraid to experiment. You cannot break R. If you are creating functions, remember to try to figure out a way to use indices rather than loops. Take the process in small steps. And remember that data frames are lists, not matrices.

Index

Get the eBook for only $10!

Now you can take the weightless companion with you anywhere, anytime. Your purchase of this book entitles you to 3 electronic versions for only $10.

This Apress title will prove so indispensible that you'll want to carry it with you everywhere, which is why we are offering the eBook in 3 formats for only $10 if you have already purchased the print book.

Convenient and fully searchable, the PDF version enables you to easily find and copy code—or perform examples by quickly toggling between instructions and   applications. The MOBI format is ideal for your Kindle, while the ePUB can be utilized on a variety of mobile devices.

Go to www.apress.com/promo/tendollars to purchase your companion eBook.